Lessons from
Little Rock

Lessons from
Little Rock

Terrence Roberts
One of the "Little Rock Nine"

Terrence Roberts (signature)

BUTLER
CENTER
BOOKS

Little Rock, Arkansas

The Butler Center for Arkansas Studies
Central Arkansas Library System
100 Rock Street
BUTLER
CENTER   Little Rock, Arkansas 72201
BOOKS   www.butlercenter.org

First paperback printing, May 2013

ISBN: 978-1-935106-59-3
eISBN: 978-1-935106-45-6

Book and cover design by H. K. Stewart

Front cover photograph of Terrence Roberts is by Xavier Higgs of Pasadena, CA. All
other photographs are from the personal collection of the author, the archives at the
Butler Center for Arkansas Studies, or as credited. Photo selections for this book
were made with the gracious assistance of Paul Robert Walker.

Funding for this book was provided, in part, by the Pulaski County Historical
Society, P.O. Box 251903, Little Rock, AR, 72225, www.pulaskicountyarkhistory.org.

Library of Congress Cataloging-in-Publication Data

Roberts, Terrence J.
  Lessons from Little Rock / Terrence Roberts.
    p. cm.
  "One of the 'Little Rock Nine'"
  ISBN 978-1-935106-59-3 (pbk. : alk. paper)
  1. School integration--Arkansas--Little Rock--History--20th century. 2. Central
High School (Little Rock, Ark.)--History. 3. Roberts, Terrence J. 4. African
American students--Arkansas--Little Rock--Biography. I. Title.
  LC214.23.L56R63 2009
  379.2'630976773--dc22
                              2009028740

Printed in the United States of America
This book is printed on archival-quality paper that meets requirements of the
American National Standard for Information Sciences, Permanence of Paper,
Printed Library Materials, ANSI Z39.48-1984.

The publishing division of the Butler Center for Arkansas Studies
was made possible by the generosity of Dora Johnson Ragsdale and
John G. Ragsdale Jr.

This book is dedicated to my grandsons, PJ (Paul Jr.), and Austin Goodloe, two of the brighter lights in the universe.

Boys, the world is not yet reshaped in the way I would have it for you, but many of the obstacles that I faced are no longer apparent. May the God of this universe guide your navigation through this uncertain terrain.

I would like to thank the Pulaski County Historical Society for its assistance in publishing this book.

TABLE OF CONTENTS

We were teenagers in 1957 when Orval Faubus, the governor of Arkansas, called out the Arkansas State National Guard to block our entry to Little Rock Central High, a school until that time reserved by law for white students. In order for us to enter Central in the wake of the Supreme Court's decision in *Brown v. Board of Education, Topeka, Kansas*, it was necessary for President Dwight Eisenhower to send the 101st Airborne Division of the United States Army, the "Screaming Eagles," to escort us to school.

The *Brown* decision had concluded that it was no longer constitutional for public schools in the United States to remain segregated. This decision was not well received generally by the American public and was seen as especially grievous by many of the white citizens of Little Rock. As one of the very first responses to the *Brown* decision, the Little Rock School Board's plan to desegregate schools was met with strong opposition. Governor Faubus, elected by the voters of Arkansas to six terms, did not act alone in blocking our admission to Central; he was simply the identified leader of the opposition. The governor and others of his ilk felt the Supreme Court had overstepped a sacred boundary. The conviction that the races in America should remain separate from each other was apparently felt deeply by a large number of white Americans in Little Rock and elsewhere in the United States. Over one hundred members of the United States Congress signed the "Southern Manifesto," in which they vowed to do whatever was in their power to block implementation of the *Brown* decision.

This unyielding opposition created a school year filled with life-threatening circumstances for the nine of us. And for many other citizens of Little Rock, both black and white, it caused economic disruption in the form of lost jobs and lost business.

As I have attempted to put my thoughts and feelings on paper in years past, I have invariably come up against painful memories and have had to take time to sort through the unresolved emotions of my time at Central. Now much of the emotional debris has been cleared away, and I am ready to share my thoughts.

For the past fifty years I have thought about what I need to say about my experience as one of "The Little Rock Nine." It is clear to me that I need to include my voice among the many who have spoken or written about that time and that experience. The reasons are myriad, and not the least of them is my desire to speak my own truth about that chaotic time, to leave a record for those who want to know what happened to me during that bizarre school year. I want to further explain to my daughters how and why such an experience was necessary. I want to communicate to my grandsons their grandfather's life history. And finally, I want to counter those ever more vocal revisionists who would re-write history to say that things were not as bad as some would suggest, that the nine of us were warmly embraced by the majority of white administrators, teachers, and students at Central High.

I want to tell also about my life in Little Rock and how and why I chose to join this small group of "warriors." I hope what I have to say will help explain the circumstances that led me to participate in the integration of Central High School and give a personal perspective that will add to a better understanding of some of the things that transpired during that year. I do not intend to provide a comprehensive overview of all that happened, but rather to tell my story. I am more convinced each day that telling our stories to each other is the way we learn best what our collective life is all about, the way we understand who we really are, how our stories are intertwined, what this reality means for us now, and what it portends for the future.

In writing about my life I will, of course, introduce the people who played significant roles in my growth and development, my parents, siblings, relatives, teachers, friends, and others. And I will offer my understanding of some of the more salient events that occurred as I was growing up, especially those events that seem to have had a direct bearing on my choice to participate in the integration of Central High.

The experience in Little Rock taught me a lot about myself and about the white people who were aligned against me, especially in terms of their responses to me as a black person and what I must have represented to them because I was black. The year I spent at Central High afforded me opportunities to grow and to continue the development of my personality, to understand much about the conflict between me and those who were convinced I had no place there, and to learn how to cope with a level of fear that was almost overwhelming at times.

I came out of that maelstrom more resolved than ever to continue the fight for justice and equality for all oppressed people in this country. In writing about the lessons I learned in Little Rock, I wish to inspire others to learn or re-learn those same lessons and, hopefully, to provide some reason for optimism as we move into the ensuing decades of this twenty-first century.

In America, we have not yet lived up to the promise of providing opportunity for each and every one of us to realize our inherent potential, but we do have the capacity to do so. So far we have lacked the will and the necessary commitment, but with concerted effort on the part of all of us who believe in this possibility, I believe it will happen.

We must confront the issues that continue to confound and confuse us. We must learn ways to accept and embrace difference, rid ourselves of the disabling thought patterns that keep us at arm's length from each other, and work toward establishing a just and truly democratic society. We can talk to those who will listen and respond, model the behaviors for those who are reluctant to add their voices to the mix, and encourage all to think beyond the ordinary as we seek answers to questions that have remained unresolved for far too long.

I want to be able to tell my grandsons that America wants them to participate fully in all aspects of life, that there are no hidden barriers to interfere with progress toward their chosen goals or ambitions. If the most vital lessons from Little Rock have any meaning whatsoever, if those lessons can be made manifest, then perhaps it is reasonable to hope that my grandsons will lead lives of unencumbered productivity, using their energy to reach any goals they set for themselves.

If the words I write serve any purpose, I trust it will be to motivate you to find ways to alter the status quo, to create a new and better America. Little Rock offered a glimpse of what we can be at our worst, but we do not have to settle for our worst. It is in the American character, I believe, to realize fully the words of the Pledge of Allegiance to the Flag—"… one nation, under God, indivisible, with liberty and justice for all."

1

My Moment as a Fly

My fear level that day was higher than it had been all year at Central High. On the surface, things seemed to be the same as any other day—the name calling, the pushing and shoving—but the threats from the white kids seemed more real, what they said to me had a definite ring of truth as they described in great detail what they had in mind for me. I had heard this stuff from the very first day the nine of us had entered the school. Yet this time I sensed that somehow they had found the resolve to carry out their plans to "get rid of the nigger."

It was a warm spring morning in 1958, and we had been in school since late September, 1957. There had been a lot of physical and psychological violence directed toward the nine of us. There seemed to be no end to what we had to endure. We were constantly harrassed by the white students, who made certain that we understood their goal was to get us out of Central by any means necessary.

That morning I had dressed in my gym clothes, and I was standing outside waiting for instruction from the coaches, who were still inside the gym. Suddenly I was surrounded by my white classmates; I had been caught off guard, and now I was in the center of a large circle of hostile faces. Nobody said a word. And when you consider the normal noise level of an American high school, this was a decidedly disturbing situation. I stood there in that circle of animosity, a circle of grotesquely twisted faces all looking viciously at me, and tried to figure out what was to come.

It came soon enough, in the form of Macauley, a senior and one of the largest boys at Central. He was a football player and a member of the Naval Reserve. I had seen his picture in the school's student directory, so I knew who he was right away.

Macauley stalked toward me with the fierce determination of a man on a mission. He held a baseball bat in his right hand, swinging it lightly back and forth as he approached. There was no way I could even imagine trying to defend myself; he was three times my size. Besides, the nine of us had adopted a policy of nonviolence; we had agreed not to fight back no matter what the provocation might be. What I did that day was to make eye contact with Macauley and hold that gaze as he came closer to me.

He came as close as he could. We stood there nose to nose, breathing on each other for what seemed to be an eternity. Sweat poured down my sides, and my knees shook. I was afraid I might lose control of my entire body because by then my fear had reached levels I never before knew even existed. I thought to myself, *If I can just get by without peeing on myself, then maybe it won't be so bad.* Finally, in a razor-edged voice that made fear surge through me, he spoke for the first time: "Nigger, if you weren't so small...." And then his voice trailed off. He dropped the bat and walked away.

Macauley, like some of my other antagonists at Central, had discovered a spark of humanity deep within himself, a spark he could not overcome. He could not force himself to take undue advantage of a smaller human being. For an uncertain moment I had been on the verge of becoming the subject of a coroner's report; a second or two later I was standing, petrified and paralyzed with fear, as my would-be attacker and his cohort slowly walked away mumbling and grumbling to themselves. Apparently, Macauley would have had no compunction about using the bat against someone who equaled him in size. My stature had been my salvation.

I learned that day how completely fear can paralyze you. After Macauley and the group walked away, I stood there frozen in place. I could not move. It seemed there was no safe place anywhere, and since I was still standing, unharmed, where I was, I thought I'd just stay there.

Eventually I was able to move, but it was with great reluctance and trepidation. My fear level remained extremely high throughout the rest of that day. Honestly, I don't know how I managed to get through the rest of the day because images of my shattered cranium kept popping into my mind. In many ways the psychological violence we had to endure was more insidious than the physical assaults.

How we managed to get safely through that year still baffles me. Given the dedication and persistence of the opposition, and the fact that they had such overwhelming support from the majority of white people in Little Rock, I might have bet against our survival. But survive we did, and even though the price was steep, both physically and psychologically, it was not too much to pay, given the stakes involved. By doing nothing, we would have prolonged the system of racial discrimination that restricted our lives simply because we were black people. It was imperative for us to take a stand then and there, and by so doing we became part of an ever-growing movement to end racial discrimination in the United States.

***

I trace my decision to join the Little Rock Nine almost directly to an episode that had occurred about two years earlier, when I was thirteen, on an unremarkable summer day in Little Rock. My memory of that day, like the day I described above, is clearly imprinted on my mind. I remember it as if it happened yesterday. Summer days in Little Rock were often quiet, lazy days. It was hot and sultry, nothing special about the day on the surface, but it would very soon become a permanent marker in time and space for me.

I had walked to the Crystal Burger, a hamburger joint in Little Rock where my favorite order was burger, fries, and chocolate malt—to go. The Crystal Burger was a white-owned establishment. I had been there many times before, and I knew the rules very well. The rules were quite clear actually. Black people could not eat the food they had purchased while still inside the Crystal Burger; they could not occupy any of the counter stools or chairs around the tables; they could only order food to go. Unlike some of the other whites-only eating places in Little Rock with a back door reserved for black customers, the Crystal Burger allowed black people to enter the front door but did not allow them beyond a very circumscribed front section.

This day was no different except that right after placing my order, I hopped up on one of the stools at the counter to wait for my burger and fries. It was most certainly out of character for me to do that. I don't remember why I decided to sit on the stool that day. It just felt like an ordinary thirteen-year-old kind of thing to do while I waited, a momentary lapse of consciousness, I guess. Suddenly there was absolute silence. Nobody in the Crystal Burger that day, not the workers, nor any of the customers, said a word, but all of them turned their heads to look at me.

All action seemed to stop. I felt I was in one of those images caught in a frame when a movie projector stalls or when the DVD is on pause. For a few seconds I wondered what happened. But instantly, and with a great sense of alarm, I realized I had committed an unpardonable social sin. I was guilty of a crime of huge proportions: I was sitting down in a restaurant that provided seats for white customers only! For an instant I had forgotten the script. I had stepped out of my assigned role, and my improvised action had not been met with approval from the owners, workers, or patrons of that establishment. Almost as one organism they focused their eyes on me with a stare that carried a very loud and clear nonverbal message: *Nigger, you know you are wrong. Now get up from that stool and act like you've got some sense.* Sensing I was in imminent danger, I jumped down from the stool, hastily canceled my order, and ran out of the Crystal Burger. I could choose not to spend more money in the Crystal Burger, the choice I made on the spot, but inside I felt like I had just been swatted away like one of the flies circling around inside the restaurant.

I was almost physically sick at the thought of what had happened. What was I to do with that feeling? What kind of response should I have made? Did I have any rights at all? What would it take for me to be treated like a real human being? I walked home that day on the verge of tears, full of despair and hopelessness, ashamed of my own powerlessness, wondering yet again if this was the only kind of life I could expect to live in Little Rock.

It's strange, you know. I had obeyed the laws of segregation without real complaint until that moment in the Crystal Burger. Before then I had cooperated with the system and hadn't made a real fuss in the face of whatever demeaning action took place. I would dutifully take my seat in the back of the bus and would tolerate the disrespectful tone and actions of the white bus drivers if by chance one of them felt that I was moving too slowly in giving up my seat to a white rider. I would pick up my change from store counters thrown there by white clerks who refused to touch my hand. But this time something happened inside me.

There was something very unsettling about the feeling I was left with after the episode in the Crystal Burger. I knew at that point that something had to be done, and quickly. I don't know exactly what I expected to happen, but I knew that from then on I would have a hard time obeying the laws of segregation and remaining passive in the face of whites who expected me to take their abuse without response. Little did I know at the time that in just two years I would actively challenge the laws of segregation in Little Rock, this time by deliberate choice, not by a simple act of "forgetting my place." As a volunteer participant in the desegregation of Central High School, I would finally have an opportunity to take a public stand against segregation and discrimination.

***

Fast-forward to the year 2002. I had given my students the assignment to bring to class a cultural artifact, something representing their culture or cultures of origin. It was obvious, on the day of the presentations, that the students, all psychology majors in a master's degree program, had given the assignment serious consideration. Their choices reflected a wide range of cultural norms, customs, rituals, and behaviors. The ensuing discussions were lively, rambunctious even, as the students sought to understand more about each other's cultural beginnings. As the last student headed back to his desk, another student asked, "Dr. Roberts, what about your cultural artifact? Do you have anything to show us?" I responded that I had indeed brought something to share with the group and passed around a copy of my birth announcement that had appeared in the *Arkansas Gazette* in December, 1941.

All of the babies born on or near December 3, 1941, in Little Rock and in nearby Arkansas towns were listed in the "Local News" section of the paper. The list starts with Mr. and Mrs. Marcus Spotwood Billingsley, 1309 Main Street, daughter, Geraldine Juliette, December 1, and continues, nonalphabetically, to Mr. and Mrs. Benjamin Stevenson, Lonoke, daughter, Clara Christine, December 5. But my name does not show up in this list. I am in the one printed just below this one—the list where parents are introduced by first and last name only. The social titles of Mr. and Mrs. are absent in this second list. My entry reads: William and Margaret Roberts, 2010 Pulaski Street, son Terrence James, December 3. To the uneducated eye this may have been simply a printer's mistake, something that might be corrected in the next day's edition of the *Gazette*. But, to the eye of one who knows and understands racial hierarchy or racial structure in America, there is no mistake. Black babies must be presented to the community as the progeny of people who have no true social standing, who do not merit the titles of Mr. and Mrs. for that would put them on equal footing with their white counterparts, and the culture would not tolerate such an aberration.

Several years ago I read Ernest Becker's *Birth and Death of Meaning*, in which he writes, "The task of culture is to provide each and every individual with the firm conviction that he or she is an object of primary value in a world of meaningful action." It is clear to me that my culture was unwilling to provide me with such a conviction. In fact, the opposite was true. What was offered to me was second tier at best, not a place in the first list, not the same level as my peers, but something designed to communicate a cultural message: "You are not as deserving as the others."

When I was born, the country was still using the Supreme Court decision handed down in *Plessy v. Ferguson* as the standard by which legal and social policy concerning black people was determined. In 1896 the United States Supreme Court had ruled in *Plessy v. Ferguson* that racial discrimination was constitutional. The plaintiff in this case, Homer Plessy, had sought relief from the Court in his suit against a rail company in Louisiana which had forced him to ride in a segregated railcar even though he had paid full fare and wished to choose his own riding space. In ruling against Plessy, the Court affirmed the right of states to provide separate facilities for black and white people.

This was more than satisfactory to the white citizens of Little Rock, as it was to public leaders all over these United States, but it made for a rather surreal existence for black people. The *Plessy* decision gave explicit permission to states to segregate citizens by race and to provide "separate but equal" facilities for those not considered to be members of the so-called "white race." As a black person I had no legal right to assume that I could participate fully in civic, educational, economic, political, or social affairs. The immediate impact on my life was that the walls of racial separation dictated that I live in a part of the community populated by mostly other black people, attend all-black schools, drink only from the water fountains in public places designated for black people, sit on the rear seats of city buses, enter the rear door of most white-owned eating establishments where black people could buy food to go, and generally tread very carefully the city streets of Little Rock, ever wary of white people at every level of society who might at any time find in me a ready target for their expression of racial hatred.

2

First Grade Executives

Life in Little Rock was a bundle of crazy convolutions, rife with its hard-to-explain, hard-to-believe, just-plain-hard realities. I had come tumbling out of the womb into a world with *Plessy*'s imprint all over the landscape. In Little Rock all conceivable arenas of social interaction were configured to keep the racial groups apart from each other. The rules of segregation were rigidly enforced. I could order food to go from places like the Crystal Burger, but I could not sit at one of their counters or tables to eat; all seats were reserved for white patrons. I could ride the bus, but I had to sit on the rear seats. And this was true only as long as there were fewer white riders than available seats. White riders had first choice of even the rear seats if forward seats were filled. White people sat on the main floor of movie theaters; the balconies of movie theaters were reserved for black people. White people went to white churches; black people went to black churches.

One day each week Fair Park, a public amusement park, was reserved for black families. On that day black people could enjoy the rides and amusements at the park and visit the city zoo, which was part of the park complex. I remember asking to go to Fair Park every chance I got because it was such a fun place to be. It was cruel for young black kids to have such a place so near at hand, yet off limits to them most of the time.

When I was about ten years old, the City of Little Rock built a separate park complete with swimming pool and skating rink for black people—black people were banned from swimming in the Fair Park pool. Gillam Park, as the new park was known, was constructed on land in Granite Heights, an area in the southeastern part of Little Rock where black people were allowed to live. Another example of the failure of "separate but equal," Gillam Park bore faint, if any, resemblance to Fair Park. Although I went often to Gillam Park, it was no real subsitute for Fair Park. From the beginning, the facility was substandard and soon showed signs of disrepair.

To me, this all added up to a very strange way for people to live. As a very young person I was curious about how such a state of affairs had come to be, and I asked questions about it. I had convinced myself that Little Rock must be some kind of aberration, that in places outside this city people acted rationally and there was no such thing as discrimination.

I asked black adults, my parents included, to tell me what was really going on, to tell me the truth about our circumstances as black people. I was admonished to "keep quiet about this stuff," "don't rock the boat," "that's just the way it is," "it's the law of the land." I thought this topic was too scary for most people to contemplate. I had trouble making sense out of any of it; their responses only whetted my appetite for information that made sense.

I remember thinking that white people must be crazy. This was the only thing that made sense to me. White people seemed to be in charge of everything, and since everything was so insane, I concluded they must be insane as well. I considered myself a logical person, and this conclusion made sense to me.

I thought at the time that I had made a monumental discovery. The idea that black people would be excluded from full participation in all aspects of life based on their skin color was not only irrational—insane—thinking, but also hard to accept as reality. But it was indeed the reality: Decisions were based on race, decisions about housing, education, employment, legal affairs, and social justice.

Discrimination seemed to be "second nature" to white people in Little Rock. It seemed to require so little effort on their part to act in demeaning ways toward black people. Insulting remarks were commonplace; black adults were addressed by first name only, and even very young white children showed little, if any, respect for people of color. It seemed to me that in the minds of most white people, black people counted for very little and could, and perhaps should, be treated as second-class citizens, or even worse, as some sort of serving class put on earth to cater to their needs.

But, believe it or not, in spite of all of this, even considering the treatment I received at the Crystal Burger, there were moments when it seemed reasonable to think that change was possible. Part of my optimism was based on my own observations that even in the midst of the madness of segregation and racial discrimination, black and white people related to each other in very intimate ways. Oh, there were certainly informal rules, strictly enforced informal rules, about the ways in which black people and white people were expected to interact, but interact they did.

My mom took her catering skills into white homes where she cooked, served food, cleaned the kitchens, and planned future meals with her white customers. As my mom's helper, I went with her into the back doors of white-owned homes. We did not own a car, so the white customers would pick us up and drive us to their homes. More often than not, the homes would be in Pulaski Heights, an upper-middle-class area where many of the leading white citizens of Little Rock lived. Once inside, we had the run of the entire house, but we had to exit by the same back door we had used to gain entrance.

Black women from my neighborhood actually raised white kids, sometimes bringing them back home with them for lengthy stays while their parents were away. I remember wondering why white people would allow black women to raise their kids if these same black people were supposed to be less human than they were. And even though I had no reliable inside information about the sexual relationships that crossed racial lines, I, along with everybody else around me, could see the evidence of such relationships in the faces of neighborhood kids whose race was ambiguous and whose parentage was the subject of much gossip and speculation.

Taking all of this in, I concluded that the official hierarchy was not based on a *real* belief that black people were racially inferior, or that white people should have no direct contact with blacks, but that it was somehow useful to maintain the fiction that white people were superior to black people. Even as a young person, I wondered how positive, or at least non-hostile, relations could be established. What incentive could there be to persuade white people to give up their obvious advantages? Surely it could be done.

***

My optimism about change had another source as well: the classrooms in the all-black schools I attended. Many of our teachers were young black people who had gone away to college or university and returned to Little Rock to find they could not get jobs in their chosen professions or areas of study. An above-average number of black teachers had master's degrees which they had obtained by going to schools outside of Arkansas during summer vacation periods. And still, even with their advanced preparation, they could only teach in the public schools designated for black children. My sense was that they were angry about the overall situation but were also aware that if they allowed their anger to prevail, nothing of substance would, or could, be accomplished. What they did instead was to focus their energies on us, the next generation, in ways designed to persuade us to work hard at the task of learning and to pay attention to serious life issues. Black teachers labored hard to help us become "executives in charge of our own education," an idea I heard initially from my first-grade teacher, and repeated by my other elementary school teachers in one form or another. Later my junior high and high school teachers in the all-black schools would echo this same admonition.

It seemed to me, a black kid living in Little Rock, that taking "executive control" would most certainly include learning how to communicate effectively. With this thought in mind I spent a lot of time trying to understand words and what they meant. The "Dick and Jane" books were used in my elementary school. The images and stories were all about the lives of white people, but my focus was on learning the words. As Dick and Jane chased Spot and Puff all over the very white landscape of their lives, my focus was directed toward the vocabulary and sentence structure of the dialogue.

I developed a love for the printed word and read anything I could find. I even read the dictionary and would carry a copy with me during lunch to the school cafeteria where I was ridiculed by other kids for being a "nerd." I wasn't bothered by their teasing because reading the dictionary made absolute sense to me. If English was to be the language of communication and the basis for social, legal, political, and economic transactions, then I should know as much about English as possible. I felt proud to be a nerd!

Elementary school was a lot of fun for me. I enjoyed the other kids, the teachers, the opportunity to make many new friends, and most of all, the wider view of the world made possible through learning. As a first grader, I had not yet learned how to tie shoes, so I depended upon Moses Kimbrough, who sat in front of me in Miss Waugh's classroom. I would ask, "Moses, will you tie my shoes for me?" He always seemed happy to do it. Of course this led to even more ridicule from many of my classmates, most of whom had already mastered what I considered to be the rather complex art of shoe tying. I was not at all perturbed to acknowledge that I could not tie shoes, so the teasing and ridicule from the other kids meant very little to me, and I was able to focus on things I felt to be important.

One new thing that stood out for me was this notion of fitting in or not fitting in with my classmates. Miss Waugh measured the height of all of the kids in her classroom by having us stand under the arm of a coat rack where she would mark the spot just above each kid's head as an indicator of the measured height. I was the only one too tall to fit under the arm and felt yet again I was somehow different from the other kids. I remember noting this as something to consider: how being different from the rest of my classmates might have some value. My mark was above the arm of the coat rack; was this further evidence of my uniqueness?

My speech patterns were different also because I did not develop a pronounced Southern accent. I didn't actively try to cultivate this, but for whatever reasons, I learned to speak without the inflections so common to many of my classmates. (This was something that would have much more significance to me later in life; in fact, an administrator at UCLA once asked me if I had undergone speech therapy.)

Elementary school provided yet another lesson for me and that was about how to cope with the various styles each teacher used in his or her approach to students. I remember a disturbing incident in my fourth-grade class that caused me no small amount of anguish. The teacher had asked us to stand and say our names aloud so that we could be formally introduced to each other. My first thought was that we all knew each other already. But the teacher's explanation was that we needed to learn how to behave in social situations and a part of that was learning how to meet other people in formal ways.

When Benny Johnson stood and spoke his name, the teacher interrupted and said to him, "Your name is not Benny!" This was a shock to all of us who knew Benny. According to the teacher, Benny's parents were ignorant of the fact that Benny was just a familiar form of Benjamin. She said that his real name was not Benny, but Benjamin. As I looked around at my classmates, I can't remember even one who expressed the slightest agreement with the teacher's assessment, but we all shared the shame and embarrassment that Benny felt. The teacher had just called his parents ignorant and implied that Benny did not know his own name. We were obedient students and would never have dared to question the teacher's logic or her approach, but I made a mental note that even teachers could be very wrong about things.

At Dunbar Junior High I encountered a series of demanding teachers who challenged me to take what seemed to be a gift for learning and use it to full advantage. Miss Zerita Tate, in mathematics, taught us secrets about numbers and their relationships to one another. She made algebra and geometry understandable and fun. And she never missed an opportunity to teach us about life in general. Each day on the blackboard she would have a message in chalk for us to absorb. One I still remember read: "He who thinks by the inch, and talks by the yard, should be removed by the foot." I would be willing to swear that Miss Tate owned only two dresses; she would wear one of the two every other day and she seemed quite content to do so. She seemed to me totally dedicated to teaching us mathematics. She was not interested in fashion or owning a wide variety of outfits, but she was interested in our learning about math.

In English class Mr. Thomas Foster gently encouraged us to go beyond the ordinary in our quest to learn the intricacies of the language. I was teased a lot by my classmates for reading the dictionary, but Mr. Foster saw merit in it. He assigned poetry for us to commit to memory and recite in front of the class. There was a time when I knew every syllable of "A Leak In The Dike," having accepted a challenge from Mr. Foster, who said that a boy in a previous year's class had memorized the poem and given a mistake-free rendition of it in class.

There was Mr. Joe Elston, whom we all called "Big Red" when he wasn't around. Mr. Elston rarely smiled, but he saw to it that we learned as much as he could teach us about things scientific. Gossip among the student body was that Mr. Elston was frustrated because he could not obtain a position as a scientist—the work he had studied for. This was not an uncommon plight for many college- and university-trained African-American professionals in Little Rock. He seemed to be angrier about this than most of the high school teachers in the same situation, and we students were often on the receiving end of his angry verbal outbursts. He told us this was deliberate, that he meant to light a fire under us to motivate us to succeed.

Mrs. Cleon Dozzell, on the other hand, offered us counsel and guidance about life issues as well as instruction in literature. She motivated us to succeed with gentle encouragement.

My seventh-grade homeroom teacher, Mrs. Thelma Dozier, would close and lock the door each morning prior to giving us lectures about comportment, appearance, manners, and behavior. Our teachers encouraged us also to pay close attention to the lessons in Negro History, a required course at Dunbar, in which we learned all about black people who had made significant contributions to American society including Carter G. Woodson, the historian with an earned Ph.D. from Harvard University, whose efforts led to the eventual establishment of Black History Month.

Most of our teachers treated us as if we were members of one big family: They were the parents, and we were expected to be obedient children. Not that we obeyed completely. There were moments when the whole structure was threatened by the actions of a few students who resisted the guiding hands of the teachers and administrators. As might be expected in any social group, there were some kids at Dunbar who chose to engage in what I have come to label as "lower social order behavior." They would neglect their studies in favor of pursuing pleasure. They would use obscene and profane language especially as expressions of anger or displeasure. And they saw fighting as a useful and necessary activity. The social structure was resilient, however, and these students were rather quickly contained. The teaching staff was particularly vigilant about identifying such students because they felt all black people would be judged by whites according to the actions of those students who acted in "common" ways.

The primary father figure at Dunbar was Mr. Leroy M. Christophe, the principal. He was a no-nonsense administrator who found time to interact with students in the hallways and at school social events and sports activities. He shot a basketball from half-court during at least one basketball half-time every year that I can remember, and he would make the shot each time. It was one of my fantasies to be able to do that, to have the confidence to make such a shot, even to attempt it for that matter.

Mr. Christophe and the teachers who shared the responsibility for our education were not only concerned with our success as students in their specific disciplines, but in our success as human beings. Ernie Green's mother, Mrs. Lothaire Green, and her sister, Mrs. Treopia Gravelly, were two of the most respected teachers at Dunbar. They cared about who we were and what we were doing, or not doing, and encouraged us not to stray from the accepted norms of behavior and performance. I remember hearing often that how we behaved had a big impact on how others, especially white people, regarded us.

At Dunbar I found the nerve to speak in public. In the school auditorium we had those bigheaded chrome microphones with metal stands, and it was my task one day to preside at an assembly just after having been elected student body president in my eighth-grade year. The microphone was next to a podium just close enough for my knees to bump against the stand, and while my voice quavered as if someone were shaking me, my knees tapped out a rhythm on the microphone stand that amplified and broadcast my fear and stage fright to everybody in the auditorium. But I went ahead and did what I was supposed to do. I welcomed the students, led them in reciting the Pledge of Allegiance, singing the "Star-Spangled Banner" and "Lift Every Voice and Sing." Then I made some announcements and introduced Principal Christophe. When he had addressed the students, I thanked them for paying attention and dismissed them back to class. After the assembly was over, I figured if this experience hadn't killed me, I could probably learn, with more practice, how to face a group and speak in intelligible sentences without causing myself too much distress.

Talking was one thing—singing, quite another. In that same year I was assigned a solo part in a choral presentation. When my cue came, I could only stare out over the audience, petrified with fear. No sound whatsoever could be coaxed through my frozen vocal cords. The music teacher did indeed want to kill me and threw sheets of music at me when we returned to the music room after the assembly. Her frustration was visibly greater than mine, but I can assure you, I felt a burning shame and wanted nothing more than to hide somewhere and forget the whole experience. Such calamities notwithstanding, I used these opportunities to build confidence in my abilities to address large groups of people and eventually to sing solos!

I was totally mesmerized by numbers and once Miss Tate explained that mathematics could teach me all about logical reasoning, I was hooked for life. I was called "professor" and "brain" by some of the kids in school, but I didn't sense hostility from them, just wonderment about someone fascinated by things that did not make as much sense to them. I enjoyed the learning process and could see clearly why education was so important. Education, I learned, was the doorway to the universe of options. Having access to options gives you more ways to respond to life's demands, more ways of understanding what is happening around you, more information about how to realize the potential that is yours to develop. And surely with education I could find a way to resolve the dilemma of racial segregation and discrimination. It seemed possible.

School gave me something else as well. It was in school that I learned about the power of positive regard and its relationship to learning. From the time I stepped into my first-grade class at Gibbs

Elementary School, I have been captivated by all things related to the learning process, and this is due in no small measure to the way the teachers embraced us. Miss Waugh, the first-grade teacher who first talked to us about being "executives in charge of our own education," communicated very clearly her own love of learning as we sat there in front of her and soaked up all she had to offer. She made it obvious to us that we were her main concern, that our well-being was her primary consideration, that she loved us. It was the kind of beginning learning experience that all school children, not just black children, should have. There, in the midst of the segregated reality of our lives, we were able to focus our attention on acquiring the tools of learning. Few of the horrors of discrimination were evident inside the classroom as we applied ourselves to mastering the rudiments of reading, writing, and arithmetic. Miss Waugh was the first to let me know that learning was my job, and that job required that I pay attention to what she had to teach me.

This attitude of patient guidance was the same with the other teachers, and I quickly came to realize the importance of knowledge. I wanted to know about everything around me. My teachers made me see how reading and developing a facility with English would aid me in my learning—and how much fun the whole process could be. What they did, much to their credit, was put all their energy into helping their students to excel in school and outside of school. Even as we learned to master the fundamentals of the academic curriculum, our teachers worked hard to teach us what it would take for us to successfully navigate the racist terrain of these United States.

Miss Waugh and her elementary school teacher colleagues, especially Miss Roundtree who also taught first grade, worked hard to instill in us the virtue of learning and the importance of education. And school was a fun place to be. There was an atmosphere of solidarity, and I felt loved and accepted by everybody there. Each and every time I stepped onto the campus at Gibbs Elementary, Dunbar

Junior High, or Horace Mann High School, I felt loved, wanted, and embraced as a person of worth and value.

It was at Gibbs that I first encountered teachers who would pull me aside and say, "You have great potential; pay attention and learn as much as you can." In junior high school my being elected student body president was testament to the esteem of my fellow students. This was, as I mentioned, in my eighth-grade year, and I remember one of my teachers asking why I had not fared so well in the race for eighth-grade class president. She had not yet learned that I had already been voted in as student body president. This was one of many positive messages I received while I was at Dunbar. This teacher's high expectations, communicated in her concern that I seemed to have been overlooked in the voting for class president, told me not only that she cared but that she wanted the very best for me.

I spent only one year, my tenth-grade year, at Horace Mann High, the all-black high school in Little Rock. But even that year was one filled with support from faculty and students. I was continually encouraged to develop my academic talents.

I was voted into the National Honor Society that year. However, I did not make the basketball team. I had tried out for the team and was doing as well as I could, but I was no match for the real players at Mann. One day the coach said to us, "Today we separate the sheep from the goats." I wound up with the goats when I was unable to keep up with the best players. But even this experience proved to be a very positive one for me. The coach was not at all demeaning. He told me that if I wanted to work hard at it, I could probably turn out to be a good basketball player after all. He may have been serious, but I knew there was no way on earth for me to catch up with my more athletic and talented peers who were experts on the basketball court.

I figured I could probably do a bit better on the football field, but I could not persuade my parents (read *my mother*) to give me permission to try out for the team. My mom told me firmly, "You will get hurt, and I will not sign away your life." Oh, she had other things to say as well: I was "too skinny," I needed to "focus on school work," and there was "no future in my playing football." She countered any and every argument I could make for being allowed to wear the purple and gold Bearcats uniform. In spite of my mom's caution, I got injured anyway, though not severely, playing sandlot football without any protective gear.

The positive messages and encouragement I received at school were repeated by people in my community, and this gave them even more weight and meaning. This group support was invaluable and helped me to build a strong sense of self. Adults in my all-black world would say things like "Boy, get your education." This would come also from people who had not gotten much formal education themselves; they too knew the worth of education. There was the overall awareness that education had real value, that somehow having an education would change things for me and I would be able to cope better with life and all of its demands.

The education they talked about included a lot more than what I might get by going to school. Much value was placed on "common sense" learning. This aspect of the "village" was worth its weight in gold. One very strong proponent of common sense learning was Mrs. Dozier, the seventh-grade homeroom teacher I mentioned earlier. She would lock the door to our classroom each morning when we were all present and accounted for and talk frankly to all of us about being responsible citizens. She would tell us that our behavior was an indicator of how much we understood our role as citizens of a society. She said, "Good citizens do not litter, they do not spit on the sidewalk, they do not speak in loud voices in public places, and they do not treat each other with disrespect. If you act like heathens, people will think you are heathens."

Mrs. Dozier would visually inspect our attire each day, and if she saw something that did not meet what she considered to be appropriate dress for school, she would send the student home to change. She talked to us about being responsible sexual beings as well, and I don't think she ever sought parental permission to do so. Her message to the girls was, "Keep your skirts down and your panties on," and to us boys she said, "Keep your pants on and zipped up." She was not afraid to address the reality that we needed guidance about how to express our sexuality. As with other things she talked to us about, she stressed self-discipline and responsible choices in how we behaved as sexual human beings.

One morning just before the homeroom bell sounded, a fight erupted in the hallway. Two boys were being egged on by the bystanders who shouted instructions and offered unsolicited advice to the combatants about how to conduct the fight. Mrs. Dozier walked up just as one of the onlookers yelled, "Nigger's got a chair! Nigger's got a chair!"

I remember the stunned look on her face as she witnessed this scene. Quickly she intervened and broke up the fight. Then she herded her students into the classroom and sent the rest of the students to their own homerooms. It took several minutes for her just to compose herself enough to speak to us, and when she did she very calmly explained to us the great difference between what had happened in the hallway and what she dreamed about and imagined for us.

She spoke to us that morning about the need for us to make wise and healthy choices in life, to consider at every moment the consequences of our actions. The choice to fight in a school hallway, the sheer audacity of desecrating an institution of higher learning, for bystanders to encourage such utter nonsense, this was, in her mind, one of the worst things she could possibly imagine.

She spent several minutes talking to us about the use of the word *nigger*. To her, anyone who used this term was agreeing to remain on the lower levels of human existence. To identify oneself or another human being as a *nigger* was to communicate to the world that white people were right: that all black people were just *niggers*, so why bother trying to treat them in any other way? She pleaded with us to think seriously about what she was saying and reminded us of the need to become responsible citizens.

I remember the disappointed look on her face that morning. I resolved at that point to make even greater efforts to pay close attention to my behavior.

3

A Minister Who Learned the Wrong Lesson

Church was another place where I learned much about life and how to respond to it. Having a belief in God was no small asset in the midst of the turmoil and confusion that surrounded us.

Prayer was a constant outlet for me. I trusted not so much in my own powers, but relied on a loving, concerned God to guide me through each day. Looking back, I know now that my understanding of God in those days was rudimentary. I had no real grasp of the meaning or awareness of the presence of a living God, but I did believe, to the extent I was capable of believing, in the fact of a God. It really wasn't such a stretch since everybody I knew held such a belief. The South is called the "Bible belt" for good reason. I would have been a truly unusual member of my community if I had not accepted the existence and omnipresence of a God who would give me whatever I needed in any circumstance. In one sense, then, it was easy for me to step boldly into the corridors of Central High School because I was armed with the knowledge that God was my benevolent protector.

I did not make a big noise about my belief in God at the time, although there is a film clip in one of the *Eyes On The Prize* (the 14-hour PBS series which aired in 2006) segments where I introduce myself as a member of the Seventh-Day Adventist Church. All nine of us had gone to the home of Daisy and L.C. Bates for Thanksgiving dinner, and the cameras were rolling. Daisy Bates was the state president of the Arkansas conference of the NAACP and a very actively involved supporter of the nine of us. That was a "scripted" affair, one where the nine of us were "on public view." It was one of the few public pronouncements I made of any religious affiliation. I must add here that I did not then, nor do I now, equate religion with spirituality. To me, religion has to do with organized churches and all that pertains to their operation and maintenance while spirituality speaks to one's hunger to know God. In fact, one of the vital lessons I learned in Little Rock had to do with some of the complexities of things spiritual. I learned, for instance, that many churchgoers lived by the rules of religion, but doing so did not require that they understand spirituality. But there is, in fact, a real need for all of us to understand the spiritual dimension of life; for as we are physical, mental, social, and psychological beings, we are also spiritual in nature. And while the concept may defy accurate definition, the mere fact that billions of people around the world are actively engaged in some kind of spiritual pursuit lends credence to the idea.

Religion, and going to church, played a large part in my life in Little Rock. In church I learned much about Christian principles, and these principles were reinforced as I interacted with black community members who were mostly members of Christian church communities as well, both Protestant and Catholic. I learned about the Golden Rule there as I had learned at home, "Do unto others as you would have them do unto you," and I remained captivated totally by the logic it contained. It made sense to only do things to others that I would want done to me in return. The Ten Commandments resonated with me as well. They were presented in the context of a loving God who wants us to do those things that will keep us healthy and free from the burdens of sin.

As a member of the Seventh-Day Adventist Church, I had difficulty with the fact that we went to church on Saturday. The majority of my friends were members of churches with services on

Sunday. The SDA congregation was small in comparison to most of the Sunday churches, and there was only a handful of young people there to interact with. To resolve this dilemma of having so few friends at the SDA Church, I went to church on both Saturdays and Sundays for many years. On Saturdays I would join the worship service at my church, and on Sundays I would show up at Mt. Zion Baptist, Wesley Chapel Methodist, Bethel African Methodist Episcopal, or some other black church.

At the time I entered Central High I was a baptized member of the Shiloh Seventh-Day Adventist Church in Little Rock, an SDA Church for black people only. Like other religious bodies, the SDAs maintained separate churches for black people and white people. And while it might be assumed that the church was supportive of my role in the desegregation efforts, I was told bluntly by the SDA minister, "You know you have no business up there at Central; but as long as you are there, you might as well stay." At fifteen I was not sophisticated enough to figure out what that was all about, and it was probably just as well. To be truthful, I don't think I understand it even now. Fortunately, we had the unqualified support of other black ministers and congregations in Little Rock. In fact the black church offered constant encouragement.

On one of my Sunday visits to another church, the minister of the church decided to test my knowledge of the Bible. He knew that members of the SDA Church were regarded as "people of the Bible" who prided themselves on knowing a lot about the contents of both the Old and New Testaments, and he wanted to see how I measured up. At least that's what I thought at first. As it turned out, he was simply using the occasion to show those who gathered around us that my biblical IQ was substandard and that perhaps all SDAs were perpetuating a lie: that they really knew very little about the Bible. He asked me, "Mr. Roberts, tell us why Moses had to run away from Egypt and hide out in the desert." He seemed happy to win his point when

I, a member of the SDA Church, was unable to answer his question. Of course it was an unfair test: I was a kid seeking to be in the company of friends my age, and he was an adult minister who, even though he understood why Moses fled to Goshen, he understood very little about kindness, love, and true spirituality. At least that was the way it seemed to me.

Like school, my church was a segregated place which offered respite from the tensions of the larger society. Once each week, at least, we could shelter ourselves inside the walls of the church, resting comfortably in the all-inclusive, loving arms of Jesus. As we sang our Seventh-Day Adventist hymns, read our scriptures, and prayed our prayers, white people were pushed to the edges of our collective consciousness. For a brief time, we could relax our vigilant postures and attend to the words spoken by the ministers. And while far too many of the sermons were scathing rebukes about our tendencies to stray from the paths of righteousness, there were moments when the power of God's love seemed to envelop the entire congregation and infuse all of us with hope: the hope that real change was imminent. Those moments were far too few since the ministers and deacons seemed to be overly concerned about our sinful behavior. In the Seventh-Day Adventist Church it didn't take much for one to merit the label of "sinner" or "backslider" or some other appelation that placed you outside the "chosen."

It was through watching my mom act out Christian principles in her daily life that I learned the true value of spirituality. She was able to communicate through her accepting nature and generous spirit how to treat people as equals and with respect no matter how they presented themselves to her. These lessons were invaluable to me and they helped to make real the scriptural admonition to love others as you love yourself.

Often, though, I saw behaviors in church that did not reflect these principles of love and acceptance. People who did not measure up to the accepted SDA standards were treated with disdain. As a very young boy I was confused at first because, as I read the scriptures, especially the four Gospels, and then witnessed the behavior of some of the church members, there seemed to something amiss. The message from the Gospels seemed to me to encourage, perhaps even demand, that other people be treated with the utmost respect. Members of the SDA Church generally did not smoke cigarettes, drink alcoholic beverages, play cards, or wear what was described as provocative clothing, and the women did not wear makeup or jewelry. When visitors showed up at church, however, they were not made to feel welcome if it were known or suspected that they engaged in any of these behaviors. My understanding of Christianity from my mom was that all people were to be accepted and not judged. So the church members' reactions were puzzling to me.

There was one extremely embarassing moment for me that was directly related to my confusion about how I was to conduct myself as a member of the SDA Church. One day I was at the home of a friend who lived a few doors down the street from me. We were in his living room playing a card game on the couch when the doorbell rang. My friend answered the door and I saw that the SDA Bible Worker had arrived to make a home visit. In a panic I overturned the couch cushion to hide the cards. I sat there pretending to be the picture of innocence. I remember my racing heart and my fear that somehow the Bible Worker had already witnessed my sinful behavior. Card playing was high on the list of things that could land you in real trouble with God. I was concerned that she would report me and I would wind up spending eternity in the burning fires of hell.

Looking back on that incident I see the absurdity of it. Nobody I knew led a perfect life; everybody was a mass of contradictions. Eventually I learned how not to worry about the judgments of other people, whether they were voiced as part of "Christian concern" about my eternal soul or not.

One example of this for me was the reaction of the husband of one of the upstanding church members to his censure by the church. He owned a liquor store on the corner of Wright Avenue and High Street (now Martin Luther King Jr. Drive), one block west of the SDA church building which was on the corner of Wright Avenue and Pulaski Street. He knew that the church members, including his wife, saw him as a sinner because he sold alcoholic beverages. Yet he didn't appear to be insulted and gave fairly generous donations to the church! Which, by the way, the church did not refuse. I saw in his response something valuable for me to embrace. I learned that I needed to make my own decisions about how I would live my life without giving undue consideration to how others might interpret or judge my actions.

4

Saved by the West Ninth Street Taxi

The very fact that a nation would ratify the *Plessy* decision that supported and helped to maintain a legal and social system so oppressive and demeaning to black people is simply unthinkable. This was an outrageous, inhumane action that led to lasting systemic flaws in this society.

And, perhaps even more than that, it gave permission to white people to belittle black people at every turn. There were many afternoons as I made my way home from school that I had to listen to jibes from white teenagers who found it amusing to hurl insults toward me. "Hey nigger, what is that on your head? Looks like a sweaty jockstrap." I was called *nigger* often, and even though I came to expect it, the word never lost its shock value. I felt violated each and every time.

White kids felt emboldened to act this way because society told them that we were less than human, that they could do or say anything to us with impunity. I was learning that the larger world was not a friendly place. Very early in my life I experienced the rawness of racism and felt the chill of being defined by whites as somehow less than human. There were many occasions when I was confronted by hostile white males in my own age group who would spew out their racist descriptions of me and people like me. Growing up as a black person in the South, I learned quickly to avoid the most onerous situations by staying close to home and spending most of my time in and around the community of black people.

Just going about the business of our daily lives we often had to contend with the racist actions of ordinary white people. This was one of the key lessons for me in Little Rock. It was not the backwater bigots or the uneducated "hill" people or the members of the "fringe element" who posed the greatest threat to the safety and well-being of black people. It was instead the upstanding citizens of the town who, through their actions, both overt and covert, presented the most formidable barrier to our full, equal participation in the affairs of the city. After all, it was the governor of the state himself who led the opposition forces at Central High School. He was the epitome of that class of "good white people" who do more harm than good by their unwillingness to challenge the ways in which racism interferes with the lives and ambitions of black people.

On another occasion, as I accompanied a female friend home from a party that had taken place at the YWCA, white male teenagers driving by saw us and began to make threatening remarks and gestures. My friend and I were standing at a bus stop waiting for the bus to take us home. When I saw that the teenagers had made a u-turn and were coming back toward us, I grabbed her hand and we ran across the street and rang the doorbell of the first house we passed. My cousin actually lived there, but nobody was home that afternoon. The car stopped and the teens piled out to chase us. We ran between the houses to the next block and, to our great relief, there was a West Ninth Street taxi just unloading a passenger. We dove into the cab and managed to escape. It was a bit of good fortune and luck. (The West Ninth Street Taxi Service was the only black-owned taxi service in Little Rock.)

That black people in Little Rock were able to sustain a belief in the higher ideals of humanity and to develop social, educational, economic, and spiritual resources in spite of the reality of segregation and discrimination is a testament to the fortitude of a courageous people. Recently I sat down to breakfast with Carlotta Walls Lanier, another of the Little Rock Nine, and we talked about how we had used certain spiritual insights to survive the daily onslaughts at Central. She spoke about her sense of being well-grounded as a person. She would look at the white students acting in hostile and unfriendly ways toward us and think, *I know better than to behave this way, but they do not.* She shared with me how she had actually felt pity for them but did not want to give the impression that she felt she was better than they were. I marveled as she talked because I could hear even then her attempt to remain balanced, forgiving, and dedicated to seeing all others as equals in this universe. Her response to the anger and hatred of her white counterparts was indeed a spiritual response. She was able to rise above the level suggested by her white classmates and choose to operate on a plane much higher in the spiritual and moral order of things. Her choice was aligned with her belief in principles no doubt foreign to her attackers.

It was, in part, Carlotta's well-developed spirituality that led her to return to Central High School in the 1959-60 school year when she was a senior. She and Jefferson Thomas, who also returned as a high school senior, had been tenth graders in 1957, and since all of Little Rock's high schools were closed during the 1958-59 school year, they were forced to complete their junior years elsewhere. Carlotta told me that the second year she spent at Central was in some ways worse than the first since there were no soldiers around to help out. But she steadfastly held on to her belief that it was more appropriate, more human if you will, to resist the impulse to respond in kind to her attackers. It was extremely hard, but she and Jefferson were determined to maintain their belief in the higher-order principles governing human existence.

Little Rock taught us that paying attention to the spirit is essential. In the face of attack, it is valuable to know that other spirit-filled people have faced such situations with confidence. You are able to make decisions about what to do and where to go with a lot more courage when you have a meaningful connection to a spirit of love and an understanding of how others before you managed to succeed in the face of formidable opposition.

Dr. Martin Luther King Jr. came to Little Rock in 1957 to meet with those of us who were headed to Central High. With him were Reverend Jim Lawson, a civil rights activist and minister, and Glenn Smiley, a proponent of nonviolence, both of whom were helping Dr. King understand the intricacies of nonviolence. Dr. King talked to us about nonviolence as a moral response. He cautioned us, however, that unless we could say with heartfelt conviction that we truly loved our enemies, nonviolence would not work. Having been steeped in the traditions of the black church, which preached love as the cornerstone of our existence, and having been taught to believe in the power of love, we agreed to practice nonviolence. We were not experts in nonviolence by any means. In fact, Reverend Lawson saw us as truly "babes among wolves." He knew how severely we would be tested at Central, and he was very concerned about our ability to maintain a nonviolent stance.

On many occasions in the halls of Central, I was witness to the power of the spirit of nonviolence. As I stood maintaining eye contact with one of my many assailants as he punched me, he would come to a point where he could not throw another blow. And this happened more than once! I think in each case the white student who confronted me with violent slaps, jabs, punches, kicks, and body blows bumped into sparks of humanity he simply could not override; he could not continue taking undue advantage of a person who refused to fight back. Or, like Macauley, he could not lift a hand against me at all.

We learned at the same time that there are many people who seek to maim, injure, and cause great harm to those who have been designated as members of some loathed group. There seemed to be no sparks of humanity in evidence among this group of attackers. Indeed, rather than seeing us as nonviolent people, they simply saw us as stationary targets.

Although it would be too simplistic to say that such people are guided solely by evil, there were times when those forces seemed to be in absolute control of their actions. It was equally clear that the love-based ethic which undergirded our nonviolent responses often further incited their evil intent. My belief in a loving God sustained me in situations that certainly taxed my emotional and psychological reserve. It sustained me in confrontations with those who seemed totally dedicated to causing me pain and suffering.

5

Finding Dad Before He Drank Up the Paycheck

My parents were both children of the South. My mom had been born in Little Rock in 1920, but she lived until age twelve in Kansas City, Kansas. Her family had moved there when she was an infant. When her own mother died in childbirth in 1932, Mom returned to Little Rock to live with her maternal grandmother, Elizabeth (Lizzie) Jeter. Grandma Jeter became caretaker for her and two younger siblings, my Uncle Edward Gill, whom we knew as Leady, and my aunt Catherine Pettis, known to the family as Lamb. Life for my mom was without frills, as she had to work at menial tasks to help provide day-to-day essentials for the family. She was, however, encouraged by her grandmother to stay in school, and she graduated from Little Rock's Dunbar High School in 1938.

Dunbar was the sole high school for black students in Little Rock and, in terms of its physical appearance, was a much smaller replica of Central High School. Like Central, it is made of brick and has a central structure with two wings, or ells, at the ends of the main part of the building. The Little Rock School District's own literature described Dunbar as, "the finest school for Negroes in all the South."

My parents first met at Dunbar. My dad had been born in Little Rock in 1920 and attended public schools through the twelfth grade, graduating from Dunbar in the same class as my mom. In spite of opposition from my dad's family, the twenty-year-olds married in

1940. Family lore has it that my dad's family objected to their marriage. The Robertses were upwardly mobile people and looked down on the Jeters and Gills, whom they saw as social inferiors. In today's terms my mom's family would be labeled, "working poor." My dad's family owned real estate, so they were a few notches above them socially and economically.

Tensions between the two families continued over the years. I had been born at home, which was then 2010 Pulaski Street, and our family moved to 1611 Izard Street a short time later into a house owned by my paternal grandmother, Lucille Roberts, who had migrated to California some years before. In fact, the home was the one in which my dad had been born and had lived most of his life. For whatever reason, my dad chose not to move our family to California along with his mom and his four siblings, so we remained in Little Rock.

In 1948 we moved to a duplex at 1624 Izard, just down and across the street from my grandmother's house. This move became necessary when my grandmother sold the house we lived in and created even more family friction. My grandmother was upset because my mother had allowed some of her relatives to move in with us. Having more members of Mom's family "living in my house" was not something my grandmother could tolerate.

Things were exacerbated even further by the fact that my grandmother mailed my dad's share of the money from the sale of the house to him at his job. She did not want my mother to have "one red cent" of the money. My dad's share came to $600, not an inconsequential sum in those days. He spent it all on a drunken spree rather than investing it in a home for us.

Throughout the time we lived in Little Rock, my mom would remind my dad often about his misuse of those funds. And yet, in spite of my dad's irresponsible behavior and the ongoing family rift, life in the neighborhood and the community seemed comfortable enough for me. I did not yet understand the social and legal realities that dictated the overall quality of life for black people.

It would not be long before my naiveté about life was replaced by a dreadful awareness, a beginning understanding of the degree to which racism had permeated this society. The Crystal Burger incident opened my eyes and increased my understanding of what black people were facing. This understanding led eventually to my choice to be one of the Little Rock Nine. But perhaps a question even more interesting than why I agreed to confront the racist legal and social system is why my parents were so supportive of my actions.

My parents were black Southerners who had not demonstrated any desire to be on the front lines of social change. They were not, by any stretch of the imagination, social activists. Clearly, we were not financially independent and were vulnerable to the kinds of economic pressures that could be brought to bear on poor people. Clients could decide not use my mom's catering service. My dad could be laid off from his shoemaking job. The landlord might decide to evict us for either real or imaginary reasons. And creditors could demand payment in full. These were all reasonable fears for us as poor black people in Little Rock in 1957.

And yet both my parents were willing to allow me to join the group of nine students headed to Central. Where they got the courage to make this decision, I simply do not know. They deflected all of my questions about their choice to be so supportive with general statements about the need to fight back, the timeliness of the thing, and the aura of change in the air. But the real answers were hidden from me, and perhaps even they did not have complete understanding of their own responses.

They were both hard-working people, and my mom was especially skilled in the arts of fiscal magic, which allowed them to feed, clothe, and house seven children with very meager financial resources. My dad worked as a shoemaker at Bottom Dollar Shoe

Repair, a white-owned establishment in downtown Little Rock. He also worked part-time at black-owned shops in the West Ninth Street district of Little Rock and in a black-owned shop in North Little Rock. By the time I started making plans to go to Central High School, he had taken a job in food service at the United States Veteran's Hospital in North Little Rock and continued to repair shoes part-time. In fact, it seemed to me that my dad worked all the time. If he had held fewer than three jobs at any one time, it would have seemed most unusual. He also worked when he was at home, mostly doing lawn work, keeping the yard clean and free of debris. His diligence about work was matched only by his dedication to drinking alcohol and smoking Lucky Strikes.

How he could work such long hours for low wages and then spend most of the money for whiskey and tobacco was always a mystery to me. As a young boy I could not understand why anyone would smoke cigarettes, and certainly for my own dad to do so was beyond my comprehension. Of course, I didn't have any of the "scientific facts" about addiction at the time, but it just seemed crazy to me for someone to inhale smoke from a substance that was essentially unknown to the user.

I took a field trip to a packing house with my fifth-grade class where we learned how sausages were made. And even though the tour guide was careful with his words, he told us that anything left over at the packing house at the end of the day might end up in the sausage. For me it was a simple leap of logic to conclude that cigarette makers my dad was supporting with his hard-earned money were probably doing the same thing. Whatever might be swept up from the floor at the cigarette plant each day at closing could no doubt be used to fill up the cigarette packages that were sold to an unsuspecting public.

My mom was on my side about the cigarettes, so this emboldened me to play a trick on my dad. I must have been about eleven years old when I bought some exploding pegs that could be placed in the tips of cigarettes. I put pegs in several of my dad's cigarettes and placed them back in the package before he left for work. That evening he came home angry and upset. He had shared a cigarette with his boss and both their cigarettes had exploded. I received only a token punishment because my parents couldn't agree on the seriousness of my action. In any case, I continued to plead with my father to give up smoking and drinking.

I was often dispatched by my mom to scour the various hangouts where my dad could be found on paydays. My job was to take whatever money was left and bring it home, with or without my dad. Fortunately he was not an angry or belligerent drunk, so there was never any fear that we would be victims of an outburst of alcoholic rage. My mom would confront him often with scathing rebukes for neglecting his parental responsibilities and for his social and fiscal irresponsibility, but none of it served to deter him from repeating the same behavior the very next payday. Every time I think about the Casablanca, a West Ninth Street nightclub and favorite spot for my dad, I mentally review the scene where I try to sneak inside to find him and put my hands in his pockets searching for money.

I was always afraid that something violent would happen to him as he stumbled home from these drunken sprees. One night, while we still lived in the house at 1611 Izard Street, he came home very late with a bloody face and my mom had to take him to the hospital emergency room for stitches in his chin. He carried a scar from that night through the rest of his life.

He and I discussed his behavior as husband and father just before his death in 1991, but his explanation of his actions was not really satisfying to me. Perhaps I was still angry with him and thus unable to appreciate his point of view. In part he pleaded the pressure of having been a black man in the South with only a high school education, but that did not explain to me why he further jeopardized the well-being of our family by wasting money that we needed, or for that matter, by placing himself in the position of being intoxicated on the streets of Little Rock.

I knew that he had completed at least one, and maybe even two, years at Dunbar Junior College, but he rarely talked about that part of his life. He had been in the United States Navy during World War II, and he had used his GI Bill benefits to finance the junior college education. He didn't talk much about his navy experience, but the little he did share let me know that it had not been good for him. The discrimination and segregation he faced simply underscored for him that even as a member of the armed forces, he did not merit first-class citizenship. He had spent the majority of his time in the navy as a cook's helper, and this only underscored for him that his position in society was always second tier.

The contrast between my parents was stark. My mom was clearly devoted to the seven of us and worked just as hard and long as my father, but she did not abandon her parental responsibility through self-indulgence as he did. Our health and welfare was the primary concern of our mother. As I said, there were seven of us: My sister Juereta is the eldest, born in 1939; I am second; next is my sister Beverly, born in 1943; our middle sister Janice is next, born in 1950. And then the "little kids," as we often referred to our younger siblings: First in that group is William, born in 1953; followed by Jerome, in 1954; and finally, Margaret, or Lisa. Lisa was born in 1957, so for her, as well as for Janice and my brothers, much of this story may be new.

It could be said that we were raised by a single parent since so much of what we accomplished was based on Mom's instruction and care. My dad did not have the vision that would have allowed him to see the vital role he could have played as a more active participant in our upbringing. It was not that he was absent from the home, but that he did not add much to the dynamic when he was there. In spite of this very obvious liability—a father who did not understand the need to provide more than occasional financial contributions to the family treasury—we managed to learn what positive things family life could provide for us.

Though Mom cleaned houses for white families, catering was her primary work. On her own, and in concert with her catering partner, Lois Jordan, she prepared food for hundreds of people in her lifetime. My two older sisters and I, and later in small ways, my younger brothers and middle sister, served as cook's helpers. We peeled potatoes, shredded lettuce, washed vegetables, made sandwiches, poured the ingredients for punches, cut, chopped, minced, diced, sliced, and generally learned to cook by observing the process up close. Mom was a good cook, and she took pride in her ability to plan, prepare, and serve meals.

She spent time diligently searching for bargains at local stores so that my siblings and I could have nourishing food and decent clothing. How she managed to provide so much for so many I simply do not know. I was there, but I missed some very significant parts. Every Easter, for instance, we were all outfitted with new clothes and shoes. We had new outfits for the first day of school each year. We had three meals every day. On Sunday we had chicken and mashed potatoes with vanilla wafers and Jell-O for dessert.

My mom also saw to it that we attended cultural events, such as the symphony concerts at the Robinson Auditorium in downtown Little Rock. Even though we had to sit in the balcony, our tickets cost just as much as the ones for seats downstairs. It is remarkable to me that in spite of our marginal financial position, Mom wanted us to experience the beauty of classical music, and she made it happen.

She took us to church, and urged us to continue long after she had stopped going as a result of some conflict with other church members. And, perhaps most of all, in spite of her ongoing frustration about my dad's drinking, she generally exhibited a calm, relaxed demeanor in her dealings with us and other people. Her message to us was, "You can tell me, and it will be all right." I think my mom knew that I needed her to be a pillar of strength for me. And I think that led to my parents' agreement to support me in my choice to go to Central High. It was not about their political consciousness or social responsibility, but about a mother's love and a father's willingness to offer what he could that made it all happen.

In our family, it was my mom who assumed major responsibility for transmitting the collected family wisdom and knowledge. My siblings and I heard many stories about the virtue of hard work, for instance. And we heard also about what would happen to us if we neglected to prepare for a life of useful endeavor. Industry, education, and responsibility were the themes that appeared over and over in the ongoing parent-child conversations. Mom never confronted the issue of sex directly, but she did find some pamphlets from the Metropolitan Life Insurance company that she gave me and my two older sisters to read. The information in the pamphlets was straightforward and scientific and actually proved to be quite helpful in giving me some basic understanding of sex. They showed drawings of male and female physiology and described how females get pregnant. And there were Mom's hints and veiled remarks about the trouble we would be in if we came home with babies before we were ready for such responsibility. This gave us added caution about engaging in sex.

Family was and is the crucible in which we could find our way, often by trial and error, without fear of judgment when we did not measure up to standards. The highest standard was "Always do your best," and we mostly leaned in that direction.

There were other times when I put myself in harm's way, however, family teaching notwithstanding. One lazy summer evening when I was fourteen and feeling bored with life in general, the paperboy rode up on his motorcycle to collect money for our subscription to the *Arkansas Gazette*. As he was leaving, I jumped on behind him with the intention of riding with him on the rest of his route. A half block away from the house a dog started chasing us. I tried to kick it away and fell off the motorcycle. I landed on my feet, but I had so much forward momentum that I could not avoid a very hard fall that left me with serious bruises and without my two upper front teeth.

I was a bloody mess as I walked back home. The sun had set and daylight was fading. The lights were already off in the house as a way of keeping the heat at bay. When I walked in, Mom couldn't see immediately that I had been hurt. My swollen mouth made it difficult for me to speak, so I just turned on the light, but as she looked at me and screamed, I turned the light off again. True to character, however, she did not panic, nor did she reprimand me for doing such a dumb thing. She called for a taxi, and we went directly to the University Hospital emergency room. Later, after I had received treatment and we were back at home, Mom talked to me about the object lesson in the episode. "Boredom is deadly," she said. "You could have died—and all because you weren't able to manage the time you were given. Time is a gift and you have to figure out how best to use the time allotted to you. Boredom sets in when you have no planned agenda, no thoughts about how to fill the minutes and hours of each day."

This reprimand was mild in comparison to what one might expect, given what I had done, but it was consistent with Mom's approach to childrearing. She always considered what was useful for us in terms of our growth and development. Besides, I think she was already wondering about how we were going to afford the dental care I needed. As it turned out, I was without those two front teeth for several months because we didn't have money or health insurance. The weeks I had to function in society with missing front teeth were embarrassing for me. I considered very carefully all that Mom had said in response to my having lost the teeth in the first place.

All of the messages we received were based on Christian traditions. Many of the instructions about how we were to behave could readily be traced to Biblical injunctions, and perhaps can best be summed up as variations on the Golden Rule: "Do unto others as you would have them do unto you." My mom was an outstanding model for us as well. She demonstrated consistently, with what seemed to be effortless ability, the value of always considering the needs of others. She never met a stranger; all others tended to feel at ease around her. She was a hugger, and if you got within hugging distance, you could consider yourself hugged. Mom was the the most inclusive person that I ever knew, and watching her interact with others across racial and cultural lines allowed me to develop a sense of the possibilities inherent in the human experience. The reality of racism, I discovered, did not have to dictate the quality of all human encounters.

Mom was polite and gracious to the white customers who let us know in sometimes subtle and sometimes not-so-subtle ways that we were the hired help, that we were not white people, and that we could not expect to be treated as equals to them. Nevertheless, Mom did not allow their behavior to prevent her from treating them courteously and respectfully—as her equals.

She did not feel the need to broadcast all of the seamy details that occur in life. This does not mean that we did not learn about such things, but they were never on the front burner. As an example, my mom stopped going to church when I was thirteen years old. She didn't say why she stopped, she just stopped.

Years later, after much snooping and prying, I was able to figure out that she had been offended by some of the other women at the church. But the exact nature of the offense remains a mystery to me. I assume it must have been something extremely upsetting, given what I know about my mom and her willingness to embrace all others. In any case, the point is that she did not speak harshly about the people involved nor did she abandon her belief in or her respect for Christian principles. My best guess is that she felt it was healthier for her to become an ex-Seventh-Day Adventist at that point in her life. She did not insist or even suggest in any way that Juereta, Beverly, or I should follow her lead. We were expected to, and allowed to, make our own decisions about such things now that we were older. And she never saw our choice to continue going to church as lack of support for her position.

This was yet another valuable part of the family experience—as older children we were expected to make our own decisions. Our being allowed to decide for ourselves whether we would continue going to church was part of the overall plan developed by Mom, who wanted us to learn early how to make decisions for ourselves.

When Jerome was born, his skin color was so light that many of our neighbors wondered aloud whether his father was the milkman or some other white man. My mom did not become defensive, nor did she attempt in any way to stop the gossip. Watching her handle this situation was most instructive for me. It illustrated what she had always said to us: "What other people think about you is none of your business." Mom always had a way of making life seem manageable. She was in no way dismissive of others; she simply knew that whatever others thought about her in no way defined who she really was.

In fairness to my dad, I must say that there were times when he exhibited flashes of insight—as in that September morning when he walked up to meet me when I had been turned away from Central High by the National Guardsmen. And on other occasions he did things which showed he was interested in what was happening to me each day at Central. He would ask me questions about the day to check and see if I was okay. But it was my mom who was able to give me the support I needed to continue facing the threat of harm each day during that school year.

Family was very important to all of us, and we kids learned early in life to respect and uphold the integrity of our family as well as other families around us. It was here that I learned the first rules of social and interpersonal behavior. My mom taught us about the fallacy of unquestioning conformity, for instance. She said that when we stepped across the threshhold into the larger community, there would be voices in support of something called "peer pressure." "Don't believe those voices," she said. "There is no such thing as peer pressure. You children can choose whatever is best or whatever is healthy for you. You don't have to follow the lead of others."

This made sense to us, and we all believed her. Because of her courage and her clear logic, I was brave enough to continue to make the choices that earned me "nerd" status in elementary and junior high school. Besides, as I began to develop a richer vocabulary, and to learn more about the world around me, it made me think that being a nerd wasn't so bad after all, that not following the crowd had distinct advantages. Mom told us what she thought about fighting, and it instantly resonated with me. She said, "Lower-order animals fight because they have no other way of responding to threats or danger. That is the only way they can exercise power and control. More than that, these animals don't have the power of speech or reasoning, so fighting becomes a way of life for them."

"As human beings we are animals, too," she said, "but we are higher-order animals. And as such, we can use our brains and powers of speech and reason to resolve differences. You *never* have to fight about anything. If you have two dogs and one bone, you can bet there will be a dog fight," she told us, "but, if two humans have only one toy, or one book or one of anything else, there doesn't have to be a fight to determine who gets the object. The two can simply discuss the matter and come to some reasonable decision."

So we did not fight with each other. There was no "sibling rivalry" in our home; it was considered as ridiculous as peer pressure. In fact, many who know our family still marvel that we had no serious fights among us as children growing up.

In our family, as in most others that I knew about, adults showed children how life was to be lived; there was little room for variation on the themes that were presented to us. If your parents were church-going people, you were expected to join them; if your parents were supporters of education, you were expected to educate yourself. Sadly, not all families in our immediate surroundings were motivated by these same values. There were parents who neglected their children and offered very little in the way of encouragement for self-improvement or development. The messages received by kids in these families were no doubt direct opposites of what we were seeing and hearing in our home. In the main, family was the group of people you could always count on for whatever you needed. As siblings we knew that whatever might transpire, we would be there to help and protect each other. Mom reinforced this by saying it over and over.

And we were of one mind about the necessity of being educated. Education was stressed in many ways from the continuous conversation about its importance to the materials and resources we were given to support our educational efforts.

Our family had a reputation for excellent achievement in the local school system, a reputation that was begun by my older sister, Jucieta. As second oldest, I had the responsibility of upholding the tradition and paving the way for the next youngest, my sister Beverly. Much of our success in school was based on our common love of reading. We read anything and everything we could find, repeatedly combing the shelves of the Ivy Branch Library, the public library for black people, to find books that may have somehow escaped our attention during earlier visits.

At the beginning of each school year in Dunbar Junior High School, awards were given to the student who had read the most books during the summer, and I made it a personal goal to win the award. Reading together was one of our ongoing family traditions, and I have rich memories of seeing my siblings around me, all engrossed in reading something of interest to them. Mom was an avid reader too, and she cherished the moments when she was able to relax and pick up a novel. Watching her read and seeing her transported, if only momentarily, beyond the pressures of everyday life was a real lesson for me. Reading, it seemed, not only gave you access to information and knowledge, but it was one of many ways to find balance amid the problems and pressures of life.

Thinking back on those times I am reminded that one of the main functions of family is to provide opportunity for each member to reach whatever potential they may have. By stressing the importance of education, by supporting reading habits, by offering opportunity for meaningful work as we helped with the catering business, by not spending too much time on the dreary side of life, in all these ways we were encouraged to reach beyond the ordinary.

6

"STRETCH IT OUT"

Support for individual growth, the quest for education, a sense of family unity, these were things we took for granted in our family. Outside those parameters, however, we encountered relatives who reflected a wide variety of approaches to life. If I were to devise a continuum with inertia and an attitude of "come-what-may" on one end and a profoundly exaggerated need to be seen as "successful" at the other, the entire extended family could be placed, one by one, at some point along that continuum.

Uncle "Tanker" Yancey (until recently I did not know his real name was Harry) was one of the most carefree individuals I have ever known. He was a house painter by trade, but much preferred the time spent between jobs, and the longer the span, the better. Uncle Tanker was hired to paint the inside of the house we lived in on Howard Street, and he stretched the job out for several months. He would request advance payments for his work and would return to the job once the money had been spent. On the other hand, Aunt "Bunny" Holloway—her real name was Bernice—was one of the foremost social climbers of our time. She took great pride in being the wife of a dentist and made certain that any and all knew this fact at some very early point in conversations with her. Bernice Roberts Holloway was a woman who put seeking higher social position at the top of her list of things to do.

My mom's cousin Ruth Lewis was a very different kind of person. She did domestic work for a number of white families, and she invited me to go along sometimes to pick up extra money by doing odd jobs. I remember on one occasion when I came to tell her that I had completed the job I was assigned to do, she said, rather furtively, "Go back and stretch it out, find other things to do. They're paying you by the hour." This was a new concept for me, and one that did not fit my understanding of how things should be done. But, she was the adult in charge, and so, with some reluctance, I complied.

My mom's brother, Uncle Leady, was the youngest sibling in their family. He joined the United States Army as a young man, and we would see him often in uniform when he was home on leave. He was a generous sort who enjoyed giving us money whenever he was around. I remember once when we lived at 1624 Izard he gave all of us five dollars apiece, a real fortune in those days. Juereta immediately put her five dollars in the box she was using as a bank. The box was crammed with money, and Leady, seeing this incredible amount of money, was on the verge of asking her to give him back the five dollars. To his credit, he restrained himself—but he was cautious about offering us more money after that episode.

Leady was a music lover and had a great singing voice as well. When he stayed with us, his rich tenor sounds could be heard throughout the neighborhood for he would practice singing in the bathroom. One of his favorite recordings was Handel's *Messiah*, and he played it often when he was around, singing along on the tenor solos.

Norma Jean Townes and Bertha Wright were two teenaged cousins on my mom's side of the family who often babysat for us. They were helpful in keeping us informed about the latest in fads among the teenaged crowd in Little Rock. If there were new songs, or new kinds of clothing, you could bet that the two of them would know all about it. I remember being very curious one day about a piece of paper they were passing back and forth and laughing about. When I was able to retrieve it to read for myself I was mystified to find a document entitled "A Nigger Ain't Shit." It was a diatribe against black people who were referred to in the writing as *niggers*. I was only about ten years old at the time, and I didn't know quite how to respond to this clearly demeaning message. But the question I couldn't understand was why my older relatives would think this kind of thing was so funny.

A large contingent of extended family members lived in Sweet Home, a small rural community just northeast of Little Rock. We would visit often, and I would have a chance to experience some farm life. The Martins of Sweet Home were "cousins," and there were lots of Martins around. Sam Martin was my age and actually attended Dunbar Junior High school when I was there. Sam, like many black kids who lived just outside Little Rock, would come to town to attend Dunbar. Some lived close enough to ride school buses and others would stay with relatives or friends during the school year.

I remember being disappointed one time when we visited Sweet Home because the Martin clan wanted to play football, and I wanted to play with the farm animals. Football I could play anytime, but having a chance to see pigs and cows up close was rare for me.

This sheer variety of family members helped me to see the value of finding balance in all of life's activities. The extreme positions taken by some family members served to warn me about the dangers inherent in living at either end of the continuum.

***

Black people in Little Rock tended to live in close proximity to one another. We didn't all live in the same neighborhoods, but we did in fact mostly all live in black neighborhoods. Ironically, black neighborhoods and white neighborhoods were very close to each other. So when I write about black neighborhoods, it's not as if white people are far removed by any means. When we lived on Howard Street—we moved there in 1952—all the families on Howard were black, but on Park Street, one block east of Howard, all the families were white.

There was an alley separating our back yards, so black and white people interacted when we placed our trash cans in the alley for pickup. And we all used the alley as a passageway for foot traffic as well, especially as we went to the corner store operated by a Chinese family.

In the neighborhoods where black people lived, all classes of people lived together. On Izard Street, we were one of several working poor families, and in the 1700 block, just down the street from us, lived two Dunbar High School teachers. The family who owned Dubisson's Funeral Parlor lived not too far from us, as did the owner of the Charmaine Hotel, the only black-owned hotel in Little Rock. My friend Allen Tuggle lived in the 2400 block of Cross Street, two blocks west of Izard, with his aunt, Mrs. Hallie West, a registered nurse.

The primary middle-class jobs for blacks were school teacher and mail carrier, and the people who held those positions, along with the attorneys, nurses, physicians, and other professionals, lived alongside less well-to-do black people in the areas where black people could own or rent property. This situation allowed for a kind of social interaction not usually possible when there are fewer restrictions on where people can live. For example, the chances for informal conversations between people who were members of professions and those who were less well educated would not occur as much in a different kind of world. Obviously, too, there were more people to serve as role models for younger black people in this situation. I was able to consider the possibilities for my life in a much different light knowing that people who looked like me had achieved so much success and in so many fields. Black people owned businesses, they had earned professional credentials, they were employed in prestigious positions—and they were my neighbors. There was something comforting about this, and I enjoyed being a part of this dynamic society of black people.

7

Three Dollars, an Eel, and Bright Kids

Almost everybody in my world was African American, and, for the most part, they tended to be kind, supportive, and genuinely interested in my well-being. I could always count on finding a friendly face if I needed directions, answers to questions, or just somebody to talk to. There were exceptions. One of the more notable was Lily, a woman forty or so years old who appeared each day on our block and was more often than not soused to the gills on "jic," as the neighborhood kids called the home-brewed liquor we figured she was drinking.

We all thought she was dangerous, although she never did anything to support that notion. She stumbled through the neighborhood countering our name calling by threatening to hurt us. But she never acted on her threats. I never knew where she lived or whether she had a family; she was just Lily, who happened to be part of the neighborhood. She was one of the neighborhood characters we could expect to see on any given day.

Another character was Mr. Franklin, who seemed to delight in "making a fool of himself," as my mom said. He lived three houses north of us when we lived at 1624 Izard Street, and he and his wife had no children. He was probably only about sixty years old at the time, but his hair was completely gray and to me he looked like a very, very old man. The most ridiculous thing he would do was to put on a blues record and play it loudly enough for us to hear it outside, and then he would come out of his house and dance by himself. His favorite dance was something he called the "asshole bow." He would stick his rear end out in an exaggerated fashion and gyrate around laughing and reminding us of the name of his dance from time to time as he invented new dance steps.

More typical of our neighbors, though, was the Campbell family. Mr. Campbell was a gentle, grandfatherly type who spent a lot of time talking to all of the kids in the neighborhood about life in general. He often gave us bunches of grapes that grew on the Concord vines in his yard. Mr. Campbell and his wife would preside over the making of grape jelly when the fruit was ripe, and the whole neighborhood would participate. Our job as kids was to jump up and down barefoot in the tubs of grapes to separate the pulp from the juice. Our parents, mainly the mothers, would then cook the juice and fill mason jars with Concord grape jelly.

Mrs. Campbell was the neighborhood piano teacher, and my sister Juereta was one of her pupils. I would often go with Juereta to her piano lessons and operate the metronome for her as she learned the notes. Mrs. Campbell and her husband exuded kindness. They were a joy to be around, and I always felt welcome in their house. Mr. Campbell was a custodian at the YWCA, and when I was eight years old, he hired me as his assistant. He taught me about the virtues and values of work as we scrubbed and polished the floors and walls of the Y. He taught me how to work and to appreciate a job well done. For Mr. Campbell, working meant doing the best job possible, the best you could do no matter what the circumstances. As janitor for the YWCA, it was evident that he followed his own advice. We cleaned every square inch of the Y, and after a time I came to understand that doing hard work and being very thorough in the beginning meant that subsequent cleanings would be much easier.

This was just one of the many helpful things I learned from Mr. Campbell during my apprenticeship. I enjoyed hanging out with him.

I learned more by watching him work and interact with people than from anything he said to me, although he did have a lot to say. In fact, adults in my world were never hesitant to give advice, offer suggestions, inform my parents about any miscreant behavior on my part, or just spend time in friendly conversation.

Mr. Campbell talked a lot about treating others with respect. He used to say to me, "Terry, it makes no difference who it is, everybody deserves to be respected. Be nice to everybody." He talked endlessly about the virtues of work as well. "Work," he said, "is the place where you can discover who you are. If you are the kind of person who tries to take shortcuts in life, your work will reflect that. If, on the other hand, you are a person who seeks to learn the most from the work you do, your work will teach you more than you ever thought possible."

In his treatment of others and in his approach to work I saw that he was committed to these ideals. He worked harder than almost anybody else in my world. He treated everybody with the utmost respect, and his attitude about work and about respect made me think of how Cousin Ruth could have benefited from his wisdom.

Mr. Campbell's willingness to spend time with me and teach me about work may have had something to do with the fact that his own son, Mickey, did not seem to appreciate his guidance. Mickey was a few years older than I and had a reputation for being rebellious and a bit wild. Neither Mr. Campbell nor his wife seemed to know what to do to turn Mickey around. Mr. Campbell wanted a son to heed his guidance, and I needed a father who was willing to teach me how to live life in healthy ways.

The Whittaker sisters were extremely overweight twins who lived across the street from our duplex on Izard. Because it was so difficult for them to get around, they would pay the neighborhood kids to do their yard work, move a piece of furniture, or run to the store for them. These spinsters loved us children, and they usually added a few walnuts from their yard to the dimes they gave us for doing chores for them.

Directly across the street from us was the house where my mom's aunt, Catherine Yancey, lived. Earlier in her life Aunt "Cathereen," as we called her, had worked in a laundry and had somehow managed to flatten her nose while using a pressing machine. Her breathing was not impaired, but her speaking voice was such that it seemed to me corrective surgery was necessary. Oddly enough, that possibility was never suggested. At any rate, Aunt Cathereen was a warm and friendly person who lived alone with her dog, Brownie. In fact, Brownie, a "Heinz 57" mutt, was our adopted pet since our parents were not in favor of our owning an animal.

The family who lived in the second unit of the duplex at 1624 Izard were the Washingtons, people we came to know well over time. Ray Glenn and Linda were the children, and we would spend countless hours with them, especially during summers, sitting on our front porches and talking about whatever we were interested in. Ray and Linda's uncle Johnny, their mom's younger brother, was there as well.

A street vendor selling tamales would often pass by on summer mornings singing out "hot tamales," and later in the evenings, he would return with a new song, "cold tamales." We and the Washington kids always had a good laugh about the change in his tune as he tried to sell his remaining wares. We would stay outside until late in the evening, while inside the house we would have a smudge pot burning to drive out the mosquitoes. Smoking out the mosquitoes before we went to bed was our only hope for getting any sleep during summer months.

One summer evening at dusk, as we lazed about the front yard and sprawled out on the porch, a bicycle rider passed by going south on Izard street. When he was directly in front of our house, he dropped a piece of paper onto the pavement. My mom said to me, "Terry, go see what that is." I said, "It's probably just a popsicle wrapper or something like that." I didn't want to move from my comfortable position. Mom kept insisting that I take a look anyway, so after several minutes of hesitation, I walked out to the street to see what the kid on the bike had dropped.

When I opened the envelope I yelled out because it was a birthday card with three dollars inside it. The card had been sent by the kid's grandmother, and the three dollars was his gift. Mom said to bring the money to her. I told her I knew the kid who had dropped the money, but she didn't respond, and the conversation drifted on to other subjects. The next day I called the kid to tell him I had found his money. When I told my mom about it she was visibly displeased. I was confused. She asked me in a rather harsh tone why I had called the kid and told him about the money. Here was my mom, who had taught me all about the Golden Rule and who insisted on treating others with respect, wanting to keep money that did not belong to her.

We did, in fact, return the money and afterwards I was forced to look deeper at the situation to try and figure out what had happened. Finally it came to me that the three dollars was probably going to be used for some family essential that we could not otherwise afford, and my mom had rationalized that it was okay to use the money since the kid was from a family who had more than we had. Or perhaps there were other even more compelling reasons for her to consider keeping the money. In any case, I learned as a result of that episode that Mom was not a perfect person either. She was human just like the rest of us, and I realized I had no right to sit in judgment. Not judging others was something that Mom had taught me already, and now I could apply it to her.

Another neighbor, Mrs. Thornton, lived just north of the house at 1611 Izard where we lived prior to our abrupt eviction by Grandmother Roberts. She owned a German shepherd with a reputation for attacking other dogs in the neighborhood whenever he could escape from the yard. All of us, adults and children alike, were terrified of that dog.

Mrs. Thornton was a most loving person. She lived alone, and I think the dog was mainly for her protection. I think too that she was a fortune teller, but honestly I didn't know much about what that meant at the time. It was just thought around the neighborhood that she was involved somehow in the fortune-telling business.

In our immediate neighborhood there was probably a total of forty kids, and we played together for hours on end. There were six kids in our family during the time we lived in the duplex on Izard—Lisa was born in 1957 after we had moved to Howard Street—and just across the street lived a family of fifteen kids. The Gilliams were Catholic and so their having so many kids was not seen as unusual at all. So the Gilliams and the Robertses contributed twenty-one kids. And with the three Ziegler children who lived next door to the Gilliams, and the two Washington kids who lived in the duplex with us, there were twenty-six kids in a small triangular space right there on the corner of Seventeenth and Izard. We generally got along quite well together but managed to upset the adults in our lives a few times. I got caught playing "doctor" with some of the Gilliam girls, and once I shot an arrow from a homemade bow and hit a passing car. The car's driver, a white woman, stopped and reprimanded me for shooting at her car.

I got into real trouble at home in the wake of that event. My mom was clearly angry with me because such an act could have had disastrous consequences. We were never quite sure what the response from whites would be in those kinds of situations. Clearly my mom was much more aware than I was of the danger level when whites were involved. Offending other black people was one thing, but offending whites was altogether another.

I typically had very little contact with white people apart from interactions on buses and at grocery stores and the occasional trips downtown, and most of the white store owners with establishments in black neighborhoods did not show much overt prejudice toward their black customers. They were perhaps more concerned with profits and net earnings than with demonstrating their superiority to black people.

This is not to say that we were treated respectfully all of the time. As black people we had to maintain constant awareness of the "line" that should not be crossed. We had to respect white people by calling them "Mr." and "Mrs." and using "sir" and "ma'am" a lot. They were not charged with that same responsibility; generally, white people addressed all black people by first name only. Any black person who took such a liberty with them would do so at great risk and put himself in danger of dying at the hands of a lynch mob.

The case of Emmett Till taught us this. As a thirteen-year-old black kid from Chicago, he was visiting his relatives in Money, Mississippi, in 1955 when he allegedly made the mistake of speaking out of turn to a white adult female in a grocery store. That night he was forcibly taken from his relatives' home and murdered. His horribly disfigured corpse was discovered some days later in the Tallahatchie River. The bodies of several other black men were found during the search. These men had, no doubt, also done something to enrage the local white people.

I felt a surge of fear when I learned about Emmett Till. If that could happen to him, I thought, what was to stop those same people from lynching me? Mississippi was geographically contiguous to Arkansas, and who or what could stop a group of determined white people from crossing the border to kill me? My fear was exacerbated by the fact that Emmett Till and I were the same age.

Apart from such scary thoughts about my imminent demise, to me the overall message was clear. Life, in the main, was full of joy and there were people in the black community who cared about me, who loved me, who welcomed me with open arms. Or at least it seemed that way. The people on my block and in the neighborhood were more like family to me than other people who just happened to live close by. Adults would act as parents to all the kids, reprimanding when it seemed necessary, or commending when it seemed to be called for. And this was expected behavior. My mom thought nothing of grabbing a kid by the arm to stop him or her from continuing some misbehavior and then reporting the infraction to the child's parents. Other parents would do the same; they all served *in loco parentis* for all of us.

In fact, many of our parents were leaders of the Cub Scout and Boy Scout programs for black kids in our neighborhood in Little Rock. We used our churches as venues for meetings and activities, and we went on camping and fishing trips when school was not in session. Being a part of the scouting program was another important way that I learned about life and how to respond to life's demands. The Boy Scout motto, "Be prepared," was like a clarion call for me. It covered everything. If I could just be prepared, I felt that I could deal with whatever came my way.

The scout masters and den mothers encouraged us to earn merit badges, and we took pride in sewing the badges on the sashes we wore as part of our scout uniforms. I was particularly proud since I had earned the money to buy my own scout uniform. My family had little or no money to spare, so I was responsible for obtaining such things as scout uniforms and any other extras I might need or want.

One other such thing high on my list of needs was my Little League baseball uniform and fielder's glove. I played first base and centerfield for the Charmaine Hotel team in our league. Both these activities, scouting and Little League baseball, gave me opportunities to learn valuable lessons about myself. Teamwork was a big part of both organizations, and I could see easily how each person's contribution helped to complete the whole. On our scouting trips, we learned the value of looking out for each other so that no one was placed in undue jeopardy. We shared our belongings, and we acknowledged and embraced the fact that each one of us contributed different skills and abilities.

On one of our cookouts I was assigned to cook breakfast and learned for the first time that there was such a thing as Bisquick. We did not use prepared mixes at home, so this was a new thing for me.

But I recall thinking at the time, *This is another way of learning about other people and how they live.* It underscored the concept of *team* for me; I thought, *Each team member brings something different to the table.* It also helped me that our leaders often stressed these points.

On one Boy Scout fishing trip I caught a lamprey eel. I had absolutely no idea what the thing was, and I would not touch it. One of the older scouts laughed when he saw my dilemma. He came over and unhooked the eel and threw it back into the river. This to me was yet another example of how we worked as a team. As part of the baseball team, we encouraged each other on the field and during practice sessions. Individual players were better when the rest of us were supportive of their attempts to master the fundamentals of the game and, of course, when individuals were better, the team was better. These experiences gave me a real appreciation of the value of teamwork in life—one of the most valuable lessons I learned growing up in Little Rock.

The Boy Scout motto, "Be Prepared," helped also as I learned more about the range of human emotions that could go from calm, quiet joy to flaming anger, often within the same person and in a matter of seconds. I could never understand why some people acted in violent ways toward others. One day some kids chased my older sister home from her fourth-grade class throwing rocks at her. They were upset because she had excelled in some school activity, and they showed their displeasure by attacking her. It made no sense to me.

It made even less sense when a classmate attacked me in third grade for no apparent reason. He rushed up from behind and leaped onto my back during one recess period, forcing me face down into the gravel. He did not explain to me or to the teachers why he did it, but it probably had to do with his feeling wronged in some way by something I said or did.

But it was not that particular classmate who posed a constant threat of violence. That role was filled by the school bully. He was the younger brother of twins who were in junior high school, and he loved to terrorize all the boys our age, and anybody else if he thought he could get away with it. On the Saturday mornings when I skipped church, we would line up at the Gem Theater, a black-owned movie house on West Ninth Street, to watch the double-feature Westerns. To make the adventure as real as possible, we would dress in our cowboy outfits complete with toy guns. This kid, the bully, would go up and down the line taking things he liked from any of us, our cowboy hats, bandanas, and toy guns, anything he wanted.

Resisting him meant that you would have to fight the meanest kid in town, who did not care about rules of fair fighting. I don't remember anybody ever challenging him or even fighting to protect their personal property. Built like a miniature tank, and evil to the core, or so it seemed, he represented the opposite of what I wanted for myself. But he also gave me another opportunity to figure out what being prepared might mean as I explored the larger world. I had to be aware of the fact that he was probably not unique in the universe, and that I needed to have strategies at the ready for life's bullies, wherever I might find them.

If you want to know the real truth, I was afraid of fighting. I was always reluctant to even go near a fight or to stay around when a fight seemed imminent. Part of my fear was based on what I had witnessed as others fought; some people my age had been seriously hurt in fights. One day as I played at the Dunbar Community Center, I saw an older kid pull a gun from his pocket and force another kid to lie on the ground while he stood over him and threatened to kill him if he moved. I was terrified for several days after that. The Community Center was a city-sponsored program of athletics and other activities for black children, and I loved going there to play and hang out with my friends. But when I suspected there might be fights, I would stay away.

One night at a school Halloween party at Gibbs, my elementary school, I walked outside the building just in time to see three high school kids ganging up on another one. Two of them held the victim while the third punched him repeatedly in the stomach. I could feel all of those blows as if my own stomach were being punched. It was not only the fighting that time that caused me grief, but the unfairness of it: Three against one certainly did not make sense to me.

***

As I entered Dunbar Junior High School I began to learn more about issues of class and skin color among black people. I had been exposed to these issues already, but I did not have a firm grasp of their extent until I got to Dunbar. As a very young child, I would hear comments about skin color, but I didn't pay much attention to them. Looking back, I am certain these concerns were present even at Gibbs Elementary, but I truly can't remember their being significant barriers for me or my classmates. But at Dunbar it was a different world. At Dunbar I encountered the term *bright* being used as a description for skin color. Lighter-skinned kids were called bright kids, and at first I thought it was a statement about their mental prowess. I was soon instructed by my classmates about the real meaning of bright, and I began to pay attention to the distinctions being made between the bright kids and their darker brothers and sisters.

The hierarchy of skin color was soon evident to me; whiteness was at the top of the scale and blackness the bottom. The lighter-skinned kids were the preferred social partners for all who believed in the hierarchy. My own skin color was somewhere in the middle, so I did not receive the respect reserved for the bright kids, nor did I suffer the indignities heaped upon the darker-skinned among us.

None of it made sense to me; I rejected the whole notion. Part of what made it possible for me to remain so oblivious to these distinctions is that my extended family members ranged in skin color from ebony to ivory, and there was never any concern voiced about the differences. My mom's cousin, Willette Yancey, had whiter skin than a lot of so-called white people, and another of her relatives, Mildred Vaughn, was unmistakably a black person.

Lavelle Davis was one of the kids in my neighborhood whose skin was very dark. During seventh grade, my first year at Dunbar, Lavelle invited a number of our classmates to a sleep-over at his house. I was the only one who accepted the invitation, and it seemed that the others refused simply because his skin was too dark for them. Lavelle had rather prominent lips and this too was a cause of derision from some of our classmates. They would taunt Lavelle with verbal insults about his skin color and the size of his lips. He and I talked about this often. "Robbie," he would say, "I don't know what to do." I was just as puzzled as he was about what to do in response to his rejection.

When it came to choosing a girlfriend or boyfriend, skin color was very important. Since the lighter-skinned kids were generally preferred by a majority of the students, those at the top of the hierarchy—those who had lighter skin—had little difficulty finding someone to hang out with. This continuum was defined even more sharply by attitudes about hair quality and texture. One could be darker-skinned with "good" hair and move up several notches on the social scale. "Bad" hair, however, doomed you to the margins. And, as with skin color, white people's hair was seen as the norm. If your hair happened to approximate the texture of what was assumed to be the white ideal, you were very high in the social order. If your hair was straight and not curly, you were more acceptable. Curly, or nappy, hair was bad; straight hair was good.

Hair was much more of a problem for females than for males. Based on the norm that straight hair was preferable, black women and girls spent an inordinate amount of time under the "hot comb." This instrument was heated over an open flame until it was hot enough to sizzle its way through the curly or nappy locks, leaving the hair straightened. The results were mixed, to say the least. The hot comb process could never create the ideal, only a distant approximation, and the pain associated with having one's hair straightened added even more frustration to the lives of countless black women and girls.

I remember well the scene in our kitchen when my sisters and other young women would line up for my mom to "do their hair." It was a good session when their scalps were not burned, but even so, the end result always left much to be desired.

Issues of class were just as important to black people in Little Rock as were issues of skin color and hair texture. Poor, uneducated people were not considered as important as people who had money or who had obtained higher education. Physicians, attorneys, businessmen and women, and others who held prestigious positions were accorded status that working-class people could not attain. Certain churches, for example, were thought to cater to the "higher classes." Mt. Zion Baptist was not a church where you would find many poor people. Nor were you likely to find the professional class in attendance at the Holiness Church.

In a sense I think one could say the black people in Little Rock were no different from black people anywhere else in the country when it came to making distinctions based on occupation, income, or class. These are American issues.

8

The All-White Electricians' Union

The world came into sharper focus for me as I grew and as I ventured out beyond the limits of the neighborhood. By age ten I had a job as delivery boy for Floyd's Drugstore, one of the West Ninth Street businesses owned by African-American proprietors. I took with me all the information I had acquired from Mr. Campbell and used it during my stint of employment at Floyd's Drugstore. During summers I worked eight-hour days, and during the school year I worked some evenings and weekends. I rode my bicycle all over the city and met a variety of people of all ages, both black and white, during the two years I worked for Dr. Floyd.

It was Dr. Floyd's custom to attend the wrestling matches held each Thursday night at a local arena, and I was always dispatched on Thursday afternoons to purchase his tickets. Since the wrestling matches were sponsored, promoted, and run by white men, I had to buy the tickets from them. As long as I was careful to observe the expected etiquette, there were no unpleasant incidents. Dr. Floyd was well known as a supporter of wrestling, and his name was enough to give me whatever status I needed to stay out of trouble.

As I think back on those times now, I feel fortunate that I was not forced to confront racism in its more virulent form—that was to come later. In the meantime I learned about the nuances, the variations, and the subtle and not-so-subtle twists this egregious way of thinking can take: the veiled references to black people as less-than-human beings, the use of the term *nigra*, the looks of disdain on the faces of white people, or the habit of store clerks to simply ignore you when you shopped in stores owned by whites. I learned that adults, black or white, could sometimes act in ways that I had not experienced in my neighborhood.

The clientele at Floyd's Drugstore was all black, as was true for almost all the black-owned businesses in the West Ninth district. On Sunday mornings the neighborhood kids would come in the drugstore just after church for ice cream and other treats. They were careless with their money and would throw it just anywhere on the counter while they waited for me to get something for them. One morning when I was working the soda fountain, I said, "You kids need to keep your money in front of you or in your pocket so it doesn't get mixed up with the other customers' money."

On this particular morning there was a man in the group who shouted, "You mind your own business. We'll take care of our own money!" I was shocked that he would shout at me that way and that he could not appreciate my attempt to prevent confusion about ownership of the loose money on the counter. He had a stern look that frightened me, and I started to cry and went back into the storeroom to compose myself. One of the young women who worked the counter came back to console me. She offered me an almost empty ice cream carton to finish. As I write these words I can see how my lifelong love for ice cream may have had its roots in that encounter.

After two years of working for Dr. Floyd, I asked for a raise. He paid me eight dollars a week, but I figured two years at that rate was long enough. I asked for ten dollars a week. He said he simply could not afford the two dollar raise, so I quit and looked elsewhere for work. For me, not working was not an option. I had to find another job soon.

As I mentioned earlier, my family did not have enough money to provide extras like Boy Scout uniforms or equipment for Little League baseball. I had to earn the money for myself if I wanted to continue enjoying those pursuits or any others that required the outlay of funds. Fortunately I found a black electrician who needed an assistant, and I signed on with him for the princely sum of twelve dollars per week.

I learned more about the impact of racist practices as Mr. Simpson, the electrician, complained loudly and often about his exclusion from the segregated electricians' union. As a non-union electrician he was barred from the most lucrative jobs. The union was an all-white organization, so there was little hope that he would ever have a chance to compete for the really good jobs. He was reduced to finding work where he could, and that usually meant construction or repair jobs for other black people. In the black community, when you needed an electrician, you were more likely than not to call "Bubba" Simpson. When I worked for him, one of our major tasks was helping to remodel the Shiloh Seventh-Day Adventist Church where I was a member.

In many ways working for Mr. Simpson was a very positive experience for me. Since he was rather obese, he could not climb into rafters or small spaces to string wire or install conduits. I had the opportunity to learn more about electrical things since I had to do most of the work that was out of his reach. And he was a good teacher besides, so I learned not only about how racism was manifested in the skilled trades, but I acquired some very valuable electrician skills that I would use later in life.

When I was about twelve years old and on vacation in Opelika, Alabama, with my friend Allen Tuggle who had relatives in that city, I faced yet another version of racism. Allen and I spent a lot of time together, and we often got so caught up in what we were doing or planning to do that both of us would forget to pay attention to things outside the world of our own creation. In the midst of some such reverie on a particularly hot day in Opelika, we walked toward a water fountain outside a gasoline service station. One of us—I've forgotten if it was Allen or me—started to push the button on the water fountain.

All we wanted was a drink. But before we could sip a drop, there was a loud rapping on the plate glass window from inside the station. Someone was hammering on the window so hard I thought the glass would shatter, and I jumped back. A white woman yelled through the glass, "If you boys want some water, fill up one of them empty cocola bottles and drink outta that. That fountain is for *white* people!"

We had walked off our anger after a while, but we were still thirsty when we came to a movie theater and stood outside reading the marquee. We had only been there a few seconds when a stringy-haired, red-necked white man with his face twisted into a scowl yelled at us, "Git aroun' back if y'all want to look. We don't want no niggers in front of this show."

I was never totally prepared for these encounters, and each one carried its own shock value along with its message of hatred and loathing. I remember the faces: twisted, tortured mouths spitting out the venomous words; eyes filled with disgust; jaw lines set rigid; cheeks burning with rage; nostrils flaring. There was no mistaking the message conveyed by these law-abiding, upstanding Southern citizens. We were colored people—*niggers*—and *niggers* didn't count in their world. Somewhere inside me a voice kept repeating, *There must be someplace where things are better than this.* I resolved to find that place as soon as I could.

I continued to learn as much as I could through reading voraciously and plunging headlong into schoolwork. I followed my older sister to junior high school and, as she continued to set a demanding scholastic pace, I was compelled to perform at the level she had established as the standard. Juereta was, in fact, to become valedictorian of her high school graduating class in 1957.

Both the elementary and junior high schools we attended were named for noted African Americans, providing us with examples of what hard work could do. M. W. Gibbs Elementary School was named in honor of Mifflin Wistar Gibbs, who had been elected a municipal judge in Little Rock in 1873. Our junior high school carried the name of Paul Laurence Dunbar, the renowned poet who published his first book of verse, *Oak and Ivy*, in 1893.

9

"The Little Rock Seventeen"

In 1953 the Little Rock School Board built Horace Mann High School for African-American students because the number of eligible students had reached a point where additional space was imperative. In this same year, Dunbar, which for many years had been the only post-elementary school for black children, became a junior high school for grades 7, 8, and 9. Mann, which would serve grades 10, 11, and 12, was located on the east side of town close to the Little Rock airport, and to get there I would have to ride a city bus to downtown Little Rock and transfer to another bus that would take me to this new school.

The following year, 1954, our family moved again, this time to 2301 Howard Street on Little Rock's west side very near Central High School. I still lived close enough to Dunbar to walk to school there, but going to Horace Mann High would mean leaving home earlier and incurring the expense of a daily roundtrip bus ride. It would also mean having to face, on a more regular basis, the segregated bus system which allocated seats on the basis of skin color.

I remember well the day the busses were integrated in 1955. Students, armed with copies of the *Arkansas Gazette* with headlines proclaiming the end of segregated seating, sat from front to back on the bus. One student plopped his copy of the front page onto the bus driver's lap to make sure he understood this new reality. All of us were more than happy about this development since we were tired of having to give up our seats to white passengers.

The tenth-grade year I spent at Horace Mann was the only year I would attend a segregated high school in Little Rock. In many ways the Mann experience was a continuation of life as it had been at Dunbar. Anybody who served in any capacity at Horace Mann was African American, and I felt the same sense of family I had felt in elementary and junior high school. Mr. Ransom, the music teacher we called "Pear Shape" when he wasn't around, calmly, and without a word, reached over my shoulder one day and took a book with the title *Sexology* out of my hands as I sat reading it in the school cafeteria. The message was unambiguous: I did not have permission to read such a book.

One other thing was crystal clear as well: My parents would be informed instantly, and I would have to explain to them why I was reading contraband literature in the school cafeteria. This was the system, and we all, or mostly all, accepted the limits without grumbling much. There was a certain kind of comfort in knowing that the adults at school took more than a passing interest in our well-being.

This was one of the great losses that would accompany school desegregation, especially for African-American students who enrolled in schools with a majority of white students. There was no longer the assurance that black students would be welcomed and encouraged to succeed in these newly desegregated environments.

I talked recently to Brent Jennings who lived in Little Rock and went to Westside Junior High and then Central High as one of very few black students there in the mid-sixties. He said quite frankly he now thinks it was a mistake to have put himself through all of the negative experiences. He said he would not do it again if the same conditions prevailed and was surprised when I said that I would go through it again. In his estimation, he lost more than he gained because he was so marginalized in those supposedly desegregated schools.

Even white kids he knew from the neighborhood chose not to acknowledge him once he was in school with them. In fact, there are many black people today who say that we need to return to segregated schools so that black children don't have to confront the residue of racism found in many so-called desegregated school environments.

While I disagree with that position, I do think all children, regardless of race, need the experience of being totally and unequivocally accepted as worthwhile human beings, whatever school they are enrolled in. Anything less is detrimental to their ability to learn and grow. It just makes sense that children learn better when they are loved and accepted without reservation in any educational institution.

It was with an ever-growing sense of the evils of segregation that I made the decision to volunteer to participate in the desegregation of Little Rock's Central High School. As I noted earlier, in 1954 the Supreme Court ruled in the *Brown v. Board of Education, Topeka, Kansas* case that segregation was no longer constitutional. As a thirteen-year-old black kid in Little Rock, I had greeted this news with no small amount of enthusiasm and optimism. Since the city buses had been desegregated in 1955, shortly after the Court's ruling, I felt that change would be swift and comprehensive. This was naïve on my part, of course. The forces of resistance emerged with a vengeance.

But even as the opposition mobilized, the Little Rock School Board prepared a plan to desegregate the city's schools. I understand that their first plan involved desegregating kindergarten through third-grade classes. This plan was so obviously designed to succeed that much pressure from white parents was brought to bear on the school board to abandon it in favor of starting the desegregation at grades 10, 11, and 12. This change was made, and the board's capitulation to that pressure from white parents was a portent of what it would do in the face of continued opposition later.

As a board representative explained to the assembled student body at the all-black Horace Mann High School in the spring of 1957, and the ninth-grade classes at Dunbar Junior High School, the first phase of the plan would involve only one of the city's high schools. Central High, an all-white school with an enrollment of 1,900, would accept black students the coming September. We listened to the explanation of the plan and when the request for volunteers was made, several of us raised our hands.

Over 150 hands were in the air at Mann High School that day. The count was probably off a bit since I'm sure I raised *both* my hands. I don't know for sure how many hands were raised over at Dunbar, but my hunch is that there were more ninth graders with hands raised than the eventual three who became tenth graders at Central in the fall. It all makes sense when you think about it. A lot of us lived in the neighborhoods surrounding Central High School, and many of us walked past the school to get to our busses for the long ride to Horace Mann. Since Central was our neighborhood school, it made sense to change the rules so we could walk to school. And so, the plan was set: in September black kids would go to Central.

There was a flurry of activity after that initial presentation, most of which I was not privy to. It included screening all the black kids whose hands had been raised that morning. The screening process included review of school academic and deportment records, health records, and probably some investigation of our overall character. I was away from Little Rock for much of the summer visiting friends in other states, and my mom told me that she and my dad were interviewed by school board personnel in preparation for the desegregation.

In late August that year there were seventeen of us ready to enroll at Central. Rumor had it that the school board, under the direction of Superintendent Virgil Blossom, used the screening process as a way of diminishing the number of black students who would attend Central. Some even said that it was his intention to find cause to reject all of the black student applicants to Central High. In any case, the numbers continued to dwindle until we reached a single digit: nine.

By this time Governor Faubus, as evidenced by his public statements and actions, was fully committed to resisting the efforts of the school board. I am convinced it was his televised demagoguery that led, in part, to our numbers shrinking. He voiced fears that blood would be shed in the streets of Little Rock, and that armed caravans were reportedly headed for the city.

There was, in fact, some reason for alarm. People I knew were saying that they had experienced frightening encounters with bands of roving whites who were brandishing weapons and demanding that they denounce any and all attempts to put black kids in Central. In one instance a gun-wielding group approached a car stopped for a traffic signal, pointed the guns inside, and asked the black passengers, "You don't believe in this integration business, do you?"

For some reason all of this served to strengthen my resolve to attend Central High School in the fall. Nothing about the way things were ordered at that time made any sense to me. Legally, socially, economically—everything was skewed in favor of white people; I was resolved to do what I could do to change that state of affairs. In a quiet sort of way, I was outraged that white people would use threatening behavior to try and force black people to continue to submit to racial segregation and discrimination. While very few, if any, emotions were visible on my face, inside I was boiling over about the continued inequities and the indignities suffered by black people.

Few were prepared for the new day when it arrived. I think everybody in town knew there would be organized opposition to what by then was a group of nine black students seeking to enroll in Central High. The surprise was in the magnitude and ferocity of that opposition.

Monday, September 4, 1957, was the appointed time, the first day of school. On the night before, Governor Faubus had ordered a contingent of the Arkansas National Guard to surround Central's campus. In a televised message that evening, the governor explained his actions by reporting that he had been informed personally about caravans of well-armed white segregationists headed to Little Rock to prevent any attempt to integrate Central High. His duty, he maintained, was to preserve the peace.

His intention, as it was later revealed, was to keep us out of Central. The Guard had been instructed to bar all nine of us from entering the school's premises. And if the Guard had not stood in our way, then most certainly the angry, shouting, deranged mob of white protesters assembled in front of the school would have fulfilled that assignment. This large, howling mass of human beings gave strong voice to their displeasure that black children would even consider entering the doors of Central High.

I was afraid. I had never been that afraid at any other time in my life. Fear was a major part of my daily existence during the days and weeks just before school was to open in September. And that fear continued at very high levels after we finally got into school. One thing I learned then and have never forgotten is that fear is portable; you can take it with you wherever you go. But I did not have to let fear become a barrier to my going to school.

And it's funny how you can make sense out of things when you have an idea about the way they should be in the first place. I knew that racial discrimination was wrong. Nobody had to tell me that. I knew also that it bordered on the criminal to deny basic rights to people simply because they happened to have black skin. The nine of us deserved to be at Central just as much as any white kids. These thoughts existed along with my fear, and probably helped me to deal with my shaking knees and trembling voice whenever fear threatened to overwhelm me. I saw my fear as simply part of the price I had to pay, part of a down payment on a life free of racial discrimination.

My older sister was already settled in her dorm room at Oakwood College in Huntsville, Alabama, on that night preceding what was to have been my first day at Central High. Three of my other siblings were pre-schoolers: Lisa, the youngest, had been born in

February of 1957, and my brothers Billy and Jerry were ages four and three. Janice, the middle child of the seven of us, would enter the second grade that year, and my sister Beverly would go into the ninth grade. The conversations at home that night did not include much speculation about what the next day might bring, but instead included the usual banter typical of a household full of children, three of whom were preparing for the first day of school. Beverly and I spent time arranging first-day-of-school clothing and playing with Billy and Jerry.

Perhaps the most significant thing said that night came from my parents who assured me that I had their full support if I chose to go to Central, and that I had their full support if I chose not to go. "Son," they said, "we want you to know that if you are set on going through with this, we are behind you. But if you decide not to do it, you have our full support for that decision too."

I didn't appreciate fully the importance of that statement at the time, but have come to realize how essential it was to have had the free, unrestrained choice, the assurance and certain knowledge that whatever choice I made I would not lose my parents' esteem or respect. I am certain they understood much better than I did what the future might hold for me once I got to Central, but they were willing anyway to support my choice to be involved. I can just imagine the kind of fears and concerns that must have been foremost in their minds.

I was up early the next morning. After breakfast and last-minute preparations for the anticipated first day, I tucked a sharpened number-two pencil behind one ear, packed up my notebooks and marched off to school, which was only six blocks away from my house.

This was to be no ordinary school day. Already my parents and I had witnessed the gathering crowds around the school as we tuned in to the morning television news shows. We calculated, however, that the imagined threat was bigger by far than any real element of danger, based on the fact that the National Guardsmen were there. We didn't believe they would stand by and allow the mob of angry white people to harm me. As I walked the several blocks to the school I didn't anticipate what I would actually find waiting for me.

Up close, the surly crowd was frightening. I was surrounded immediately by a corps of reporters and photographers. The mob behind them jeered and shouted obscenities as I alternately responded to questions from the media representatives and attempted to walk through the line of Guardsmen. After a few tries I saw that the Guard's primary assignment was to keep me out of school.

By some odd quirk of fate, one of our small group, Elizabeth Eckford, had arrived first and alone faced the raw hatred of the mob in its full force. It has been widely reported that her family had no telephone and therefore she was not told that we had planned to arrive in a group. I can only say that my family did have a telephone, yet we received no such message either.

I arrived alone a few minutes later than Elizabeth and faced that same mob. The crowd was so dense that I could not even see Elizabeth as she sat on a bus bench at the corner of Sixteenth and Park streets. A news reporter told me that another black student was sitting there, and I finally spotted her through the throng from my vantage point across the street a few yards west of where she sat.

Elizabeth was visibly shaken by all of the hostility directed toward her, and I had begun to feel a higher level of fear myself as I listened to the taunts and name-calling from the mob. I made my way over to Elizabeth to see if I could offer anything that might help her. I suggested she walk home with me, but she declined. She told me later that if she had gone home with me she still would have had to find a way to get to her own home. Grace Lorch, a white woman from Little Rock, stayed with Elizabeth and said that she would see to it that she got on a bus. I decided it would be best if I went back home, and I turned away from the mob and started to walk.

I had walked perhaps half a block when I heard footsteps behind me and turned around to see a lone white man coming toward me. I assumed what must have been my version of a karate stance in anticipation of a fight, but he waved his hand and said that he was a friend. He apologized on behalf of the people who were gathered around the school. He said he wanted me to know that not all white people were opposed to desegregating Central High School.

About that time my dad walked up. He had seen the live television coverage of the increasing chaos, and he had come to escort me home. Dad and I thanked the man whose name I never knew, and we continued our walk home. We all escaped physical harm that day, Elizabeth by the city bus, my dad and I by walking home together, but the psychological impact on all of us was profound.

It's hard even now, more than fifty years later, to erase those images of twisted, hate-filled faces from my memory. On occasion I still hear the sound of shrill voices filling the air with vicious, knife-edged words calculated to hurt as much as possible. By contrast, I remember also the white man who taught me that day that not all white people in Little Rock were my enemies.

Later, while watching television news reports about the events of the day, I saw the gauntlet Elizabeth had to walk that morning. She had arrived at Fourteenth and Park, the northern end of the school, and walked the two blocks to Sixteenth and Park, the southern end, in her attempt to get through the line of National Guardsmen. Sometime later that morning the other seven students arrived as a group and were met by the same unrelenting mob.

It would be another three weeks before we were able to actually enter the school. In the interim, as we awaited the outcomes of various legal strategies designed to open the doors of Central for us, we were tutored by faculty and students of Philander Smith College, an all-black college in Little Rock. This was one example of the support we received from the people of Little Rock as we watched the drama unfold around us. Philander Smith College had been established in 1877 as a school for newly freed slaves. And here, eighty years later, it was still serving the educational needs of African Americans.

In 1997 I had the opportunity to speak at a program at Philander Smith College, and I would like to quote from my speech given that day, September 27, on the steps of the college:

> During the three-week period as we awaited the outcome of the legal wrangling over states' rights versus federal rights, Philander Smith College faculty and students tutored us in the high school subjects being taught to our future Central High classmates. From these dedicated educators and scholars we heard the same litany that had been communicated to us by teachers at Gibbs Elementary, Stevens Elementary, Dunbar Junior High School, and Horace Mann High; they told us in words chosen carefully to accentuate the message that education was important and that excellence was the expectation. (Full text follows in the appendix.)

Never once during this interim period did I feel that we would have to return to Horace Mann High School. I don't know where my optimism came from, but I had a sense that things would work out much sooner than anybody expected. The three weeks passed very quickly, and we once again prepared to face the mobs which had not diminished in force during the brief hiatus.

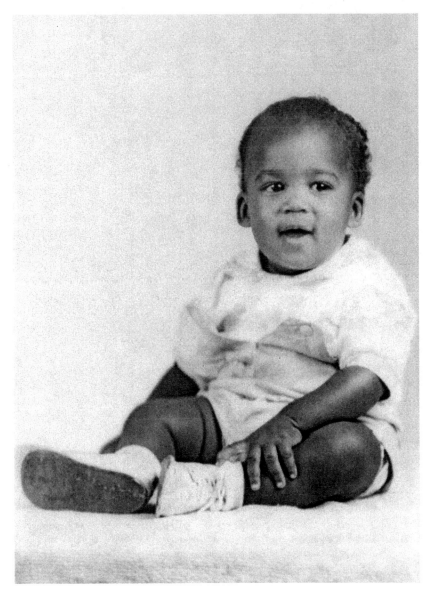

Terrence Roberts at age six months. *From the Roberts family photo album.*

Arkansas National Guardsmen stand in the way of Terrence Roberts as he attempts to enter Little Rock Central High School, where he was enrolled as a junior, September 4, 1957. *From the Roberts family photo album.*

Terrence Roberts talks on the phone while holding infant sister Lisa, 1957. *From the Roberts family photo album.*

All of Terrence Roberts's family except his father appear in this 1959 snapshot. *Front, from left to right:* William, age 6; Jerome, age 5; Margaret Elizabeth ("Lisa"), age 2; Janice, age 8. *Middle row:* Juereta, age 19; Margaret (Mother); Beverly, age 16. *Back:* Terrence, age 17; Uncle Edward ("Leady"). *From the Roberts family photo album.*

Little Rock Police provide safe transportation for the Little Rock Nine, 1957. *From the Roberts family photo album.*

Terrence Roberts and fellow Little Rock Nine members Minnijean Brown *(left)* and
Thelma Mothershed *(right)* leaving the federal courtroom in Little Rock following a
hearing on their right to attend classes at Little Rock Central High School,
September 1957. *From the Roberts family photo album.*

L. C. and Daisy Bates share Thanksgiving dinner with the Little Rock Nine, with the cameras rolling, November 1957. *From the Roberts family photo album.*

Terrence Roberts during the 1960s. *From the Roberts family photo album.*

Terrence Roberts's
wife, Rita, and
daughters Angela,
age 7 (left) and
Rebecca, age five
(right) stand in the
yard of their Los
Angeles home in
this 1969 snapshot.
*From the Roberts
family photo album.*

Terrence Roberts (second from left) participates in a panel discussion as part of the
fiftieth-anniversary observance, 2007. *From the Roberts family photo album.*

Terrence Roberts (*seated front row, fourth from left*) with the rest of the Little Rock Nine on the dais at the dedication of the new visitor center during the fiftieth-anniversary observance, 2007. *From the Roberts family photo album.*

This display case near the office of Little Rock Central High School contains photographs and memorabilia of the Little Rock Nine. *From the Roberts family photo album.*

Terrence Roberts speaks at the Arkansas Governor's Mansion event during the fiftieth-anniversary observance, 2007. Governor Mike Beebe stands at front left. Melba Pattillo Beals holds Roberts's arm. *From the Roberts family photo album.*

Little Rock Nine members at the Governor's Mansion event during the fiftieth-anniversary observance, 2007. *(Left to right)* Minnijean Brown Trickey, Jefferson Thomas, Elizabeth Eckford, Ernest Green, Carlotta Walls LaNier, Gloria Ray Karlmark, Governor Mike Beebe, Terrence Roberts, Melba Pattillo Beals, First Lady Ginger Beebe, and Thelma Mothershed Wair. *From the Roberts family photo album.*

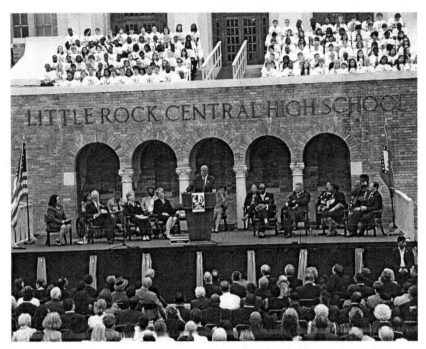

In this photo taken in front of Central High during the fiftieth-anniversary observance in 2007, Terrence Roberts speaks from the podium. Others on the dais include the other Little Rock Nine members, former president Bill Clinton, former first lady (and presidential candidate at the time) Hillary Rodham Clinton, LRCHS principal Nancy Rousseau, Governor Mike Beebe, and Little Rock mayor Mark Stodola. *From the Roberts family photo album.*

This cast-bronze memorial to the Little Rock Nine, designed and sculpted by
Little Rock artist John Deering, was installed on the grounds of the Arkansas
State Capitol and dedicated on August 30, 2005. *Photo courtesy of Arkansas
Department of Parks & Tourism.*

10

Daisy Bates and Thurgood Marshall

A lot of people had been caught off guard by the governor's action. His use of National Guardsmen to prevent us from attending Central High had not been anticipated by the school board members, and their response was one of confusion and frustration. Massive resistance was well underway in Little Rock. Emboldened by the state's chief executive, many of Little Rock's citizens had taken up positions of vigilance around Central High, adding their own muscle and determination to that of the National Guardsmen already stationed there.

It was at this juncture that the National Association for the Advancement of Colored People became an even more active participant in our struggle to force the governor to relent and remove the guardsmen so that we could enter school. The NAACP, under the leadership and guidance of state Conference President Daisy Bates, had sought to hasten the desegregation of Little Rock's schools since the *Brown* decision had been rendered. Attorneys from the Legal Defense and Educational Fund of the NAACP filed court documents on our behalf seeking removal of the Guard.

As plaintiffs in the case, we held strategy sessions with attorneys Wiley Branton and Thurgood Marshall as they searched for ways to force the governor to step aside and allow us to attend school. These sessions were held often at the home of L.C. and Daisy Bates, who were committed to doing whatever it took to get us into Central High School. Daisy Bates was already regarded as one of the foremost social activists of the time. She and her husband, L.C. Bates, were owners and publishers of the *Arkansas State Press*, the paper most black people in Little Rock relied on for news and information, especially local news.

In their paper, they offered consistent challenges to the "separate but equal" systems present in Little Rock. L.C. and Daisy Bates were committed to social change and were prepared to sacrifice even the *State Press* if necessary. I point this out because it was obvious that any white support of the paper would vanish in the wake of their continued involvement in civil rights activities. In fact, the loss of advertising revenues did force them to go to an all-subscription model. But before very long it became evident that this system could not financially sustain the newspaper's operation.

On Friday, September 20, 1957, following an injunction granted by a federal judge, the Arkansas National Guard was removed. We were then expected to enter the school with Little Rock police as our only guardians.

The following Monday, September 23, was a day I can never forget. That day the nine of us were able to enter school while the mob, which had gathered daily at Central since the first day of school, was restrained by Little Rock policemen. Those familiar with the relationship between Southern white policemen and black citizens will no doubt wonder about our sanity as they read these lines, but all nine of us entered Central as a group that morning.

Arrangements had been made with the police for us to gather at the Bates' home, and we went with a police escort from there to Central. We entered by the side door on the Sixteenth Street side of the school. I remember being extremely anxious that morning because I could see and hear the frenzied mob as we scurried inside the building. The mob became increasingly agitated, and as soon as they learned that we had gained entry to the school, they began to overpower the lines of policemen. Although I didn't know it at the time, I was told later that several policemen had ripped off their badges and joined the mob. What I do know is that the police force was unable to prevent the mob from coming into the school to seek us out.

We had been in school for less than two hours when things really began to heat up. Fear was written on the faces of the teachers and the white students as well as on our own as mob violence escalated. Several arrests were being made. Or I should say attempts to arrest some of the offenders were made. Before the mob was able to get into the school, however, we were rounded up from our various classes and taken down to the basement garage where we were instructed by the assistant chief of police, Gene Smith, to get into a couple of Little Rock Police Force sedans. Federal observers were on the scene and, in conjunction with the local officials, they concluded that we were in extreme danger and needed to be removed from the school. We were told to move very quickly, to go with dispatch to the basement where the cars were waiting for us. They told us to put notebooks against the windows and keep down. The policemen driving the cars were instructed to keep moving no matter what obstacles might be encountered.

We sped out of the garage to safety. Things happened so quickly and our fears were so pronounced that I can't even remember who was in which car that morning. Whatever we did say to each other was spoken in hushed tones as we watched the mob milling around the school. We were all taken to our own homes that morning and told by Mrs. Bates and our attorneys, Wiley Branton and Thurgood Marshall, to await further instructions about getting back to school.

***

I have no doubt that our lives were in jeopardy that morning, perhaps more so than at any other time during that school year. The mob was incensed, and we could hear the voices screaming for our blood. After we were taken away from the school, some members of the mob went inside to confirm that we had actually left the premises. They had promised to wreak havoc otherwise.

On that same morning several black news reporters, James Hicks, Moses Newsome, and Alex Wilson, were attacked after having been accused of distracting the mob so we could enter the school. I still cringe each time I see the newsreel shot of Alex Wilson, reporter from the *Memphis Tri-State Defender*, being hit with a brick wielded by one of the white men in the mob. The beating he absorbed that day contributed to his early death, a great loss for all of us. His quiet dignity in the face of raw hatred and irrational animosity, his unwillingness to run, his refusal to allow the mob to see his fear was inspirational to me in 1957 and motivates me still to confront racism wherever I find it.

One of the most important lessons I learned about racism in 1957 is that most white Americans did not understand how discrimination affects the daily lives of people of color. Many white people in Little Rock embraced racism wholeheartedly and made no secret of the fact that they considered themselves superior to black people. Even today some whites will agree that racism is an inconvenience and an annoyance, but still stop short of admitting that it is an ever-present reality for African Americans and other people of color in this country.

The school board was in disarray by this time. They had few answers for us in terms of when we could go to school without fear of being lynched. I believe they simply threw up their hands in the face of the governor's opposition to their planned desegregation of Central High School. Fortunately, in the wake of the school's inability to mount a counter-strategy to Faubus and his supporters, the NAACP had proven it was ready to fill the leadership void.

Daisy Bates became our recognized spokesperson as we continued to plan how and when we could get back to school. Daisy and L.C. had been consistently vocal in their opposition to segregation. Their willingness to risk loss of their newspaper business by supporting our efforts to enroll in Central was based on their belief that the loss would be miniscule compared to the civil rights gains with our success. In time they did lose the business, but their work on our behalf never slackened.

11

A System for Rating Insults

Ultimately it took military force. President Eisenhower was forced to call in the 101st Airborne Division of the United States Army to open the school doors for us. The president was reluctant at first to take such action because he believed firmly in the concept of states' rights. It was his position that federal authority should be used sparingly, if at all, when disputes of this nature arose within the borders of a given state. Fortunately for us, there were people like Attorney General Herbert Brownell who urged the president to consider intervening. I understand also that Billy Graham and Paul Robeson, among other prominent U.S. citizens, spoke out about the need for protection for the nine of us.

So President Eisenhower changed his mind. And on September 25, 1957, we entered Central High under the protection and guard of the 101st. It was one of the brighter moments of the whole experience. I felt relieved to know that whatever opposition we faced would be met by the force and might of the United States Army. This was a long-awaited and welcome statement that this country did indeed have a commitment to treating me with respect and ensuring that my basic rights were protected.

That morning the nine of us again assembled at the Bates home and piled into an army station wagon while machine-gun-mounted Jeeps patrolled the area. When we were ready to leave, the Jeeps took up positions in front of and behind the station wagon, and we formed a convoy that drove non-stop through the streets of Little Rock with sirens announcing our coming. Soldiers led the way as we stepped out of the station wagon and headed for the school's front door.

I felt very special at that moment. I was aware that something momentous was taking place. But years would pass before I would truly grasp the significance of what had happened. This was the first time since Reconstruction that federal troops had been ordered into the South to protect the rights of African Americans. On that morning, however, my primary thought was that maybe now I would not be killed for simply trying to go to school.

For the first few weeks, the soldiers were present in great numbers, and one of them stood outside my classroom and walked with me from class to class. This was true for the other eight of us as well. All the soldiers of the 101st assigned to Central High were white. A command decision had been made about this on the assumption that the presence of black soldiers would be more provocative to the mob gathered around the school. I learned later that black soldiers in the 101st were eagerly looking forward to an opportunity to confront hostile white members of the mob and were more than disappointed to discover they would not be allowed to participate at Central. In retrospect the strategy probably was a good one. It is not likely that black soldiers would have been as restrained as their white counterparts, given the racially charged nature of the confrontation.

We were only a few years younger than the soldiers, and I could read the lines of concern on their faces as the drama continued to unfold. Their job was made somewhat easier by the fact that several white students in each of my four classes got up, and after giving me the benefit of their best thinking about my ancestry, my skin color, my parentage, and also some unsolicited travel advice, walked out vowing never to return as long as I was there. "We will never be in school with niggers!"

I am convinced that this group would have been the most troublesome had they remained in school. They were the ones who would have stopped at nothing to remove us from the school, dead or alive. Unfortunately, a large number of those who remained took on the responsibility of trying to drive us out of school. This group of students was willing to do whatever they could think of to persuade us to reconsider our decision to come to Central. They hit, kicked, pushed, shoved, slapped, tripped, scratched, spat on, and verbally abused us constantly.

They fell under close scrutiny of the 101st, and many times I was warned by my guard to avoid certain areas where trouble seemed to be brewing. When groups of students would gather in the more isolated parts of the school or when groups would hide behind bushes just outside exit doors, our guards would warn us. I was able to cope with a lot of the maltreatment because I believed that if things got really bad, the soldiers would just use their weapons and protect us with firepower. What I didn't know then, but discovered years later, was that none of the soldiers had ammunition. Another command decision had been made by General Edwin Walker to prohibit the use of loaded rifles at Central High. He feared a blood bath might ensue in the face of intense provocation. Since such an action would have been hard or virtually impossible to explain to the American public, he chose to use the threat of firepower rather than the real thing.

In spite of the presence of the 101st, I had to contend daily with white students bent on causing me harm and injury. The nine of us had agreed to follow the principles of nonviolence although we had had only rudimentary training in this area. We had met with Dr. Martin Luther King, Jr., who came to Little Rock in 1957. And we had spent some time with Rev. James Lawson and Glenn Smiley, two men who had helped Dr. King refine his own understanding of nonviolence. But we were "winging it" to say the least. There was ample opportunity to practice, however, so we learned pretty quickly how to handle a variety of life-threatening situations. Jefferson Thomas says, for instance, that while he was dedicated to turning the other cheek, there was nothing in the rule book to suggest that he had to turn it in the near vicinity of his assailant. Jefferson reasoned that he could sprint to the other end of the hall and then turn the other cheek.

For some reason it had always been clear to me that the words spat out by the taunting students had actually very little to do with me. First, my mom had taught me that what others may say about me has nothing to do with me. Also, I had a lot of experience with this kind of thing from my junior high school days. There were some of my black classmates who had discovered that they could start fistfights by talking about each other's mothers. One would start the "dozens" with "Yo mama wears combat boots," or some other such nonsense. The dialogue would then escalate to the point where one would feel bested by the verbal prowess of the other, and the fight was on. My unwillingness to participate in the verbal jousting (and my fear of getting hurt in a fistfight) led me to develop a strategy that took the bite out of the demeaning (but often very creative!) remarks directed toward my mother.

I would say something like, "If you'd like, I'll take you home to meet my mother. She will be able to tell you whether your concerns about her footwear are right. You can ask her to her face if she owns any combat boots, and you can personally inspect her closets." This worked every time. Not one of them had the courage to take me up on the offer.

So when the white kids at Central tried to upset me with their verbal abuse, I was more than prepared. I concluded that they lacked the verbal skills necessary to play the "dozens." Although I never visibly reacted when confronted with the "dozens," I would think of great responses in my own mind and laugh to myself when I felt I would have won the exchange. I would say that my record was a winning one; after all, I had learned from the best practitioners. I also

developed a mental rating scale to evaluate the creativity of the insults
with a range of *one*, if the remark was totally without creativity, to *ten*,
if it demonstrated true genius. If I felt a certain insulting remark was
creative enough—not ordinary or prosaic—I would be willing to give
it an *eight* or better. Nobody ever scored above a *two* on my scale
during that entire school year.

There were far more serious encounters during that school year,
and I had to call on all the resources at my command to get through
those experiences. One of my classmates, Jerry Tuley, was a constant
irritant. He was assigned to the same homeroom I was in and wherever
I was, Tuley contrived to be behind me so he could kick, push, shove,
trip, or hit me. In gym class when we lined up to do calisthenics, Tuley
would place himself in line behind me and change all of the exercises
into ways to aggravate me. If we did jumping jacks, Tuley would kick
forward instead of sideways. If we played basketball, I could be certain
that I would be tripped or the ball would be "passed" to me when I
wasn't looking.

The guards were not allowed to be inside any of our classes so it
was possible for all of this to go on with only the teachers around to
intervene. One day, the coach, an ex-marine type, called us to
assembly and said he had noticed several guys picking on Roberts (he
called us all by our last names, U.S. Marine style). He talked about
how unfair this was and said, "If anybody has anything against
Roberts, he should challenge him to the mat."

Let me add here that the coach and I had not talked about this
as a possible remedy, so I was surprised to hear him offer this
alternative. Very quickly a long line formed with Tuley at the head.
When I saw this happening I thought, *I probably will not make it out of
the gym alive today.* I had no faith in the coach's ability to control the
group if they decided to tear me apart. I decided that if I did die, one
other person would die with me. And it seemed destined that the
other person would be Tuley. Since I had concluded that I was

probably going to die, I decided to suspend my pledge to be nonviolent. I was fully prepared to defend myself using whatever tactics seemed most effective.

I looked over at Tuley and thought, *Tuley, you are so concerned about being wherever I am. Well, I am just about to depart this universe, and in order for you to follow me, you will have to depart the universe as well.* Of course, since I was the only one with this information, the only one who truly understood the entire dynamic, I would have to take responsibility for Tuley's demise. I was willing to accept this responsibility.

The group taunted and dared me to take the challenge. For a few minutes I thought about appealing to the coach, but his own macho way of thinking had convinced him that this was the only fair way to decide the issue. That is, if I proved myself on the mat then the unfair treatment would stop. I knew how illogical that was, but I didn't think the coach would appreciate my reasoning.

In any case, I stepped onto the mat and Tuley was quick to come after me. He was wearing a set of military dog tags that day and as he attempted to throw me down, I sidestepped him and threw him down instead. In a flash I grabbed the chain holding the dog tags and began to twist it as hard as I could while holding him down and cutting off his air supply. We were about the same size, both tall, skinny kids, and I had little trouble keeping him face down on the mat. As Tuley began to turn blue and gasp for air, the coach stepped in and broke up the fight. He said, "That's enough. I hope now you guys will either leave Roberts alone or act like men and challenge him to the mat." I was perfectly content with the first part, but I needed no more challenges.

This did not change anything at all; it just incited more fury from those who wished me harm. A few days later I was standing at my gym locker after taking a shower (during which I had had to step over broken pieces of glass and avoid jets of extremely hot water turned toward me). I was about to open my locker door when somebody threw a combination lock from a very short distance and caught me hard on the left side of the head. I was stunned by the blow and went down on one knee while reaching out to grab the locker door handle to keep from falling completely to the floor. I remember thinking that if I did hit the floor, whoever was watching probably had more mayhem in mind.

In the midst of the haze caused by the blow to my head, I could hear the sound of feet coming toward me, but I struggled to keep my balance and stumbled out of the locker room into the coach's office, which, fortunately was nearby. The coach ran out yelling at the culprits who ran away.

After my head cleared a bit and I got first aid for the cut on my head, I went back to the locker room to dress. There I discovered that all of my clothing was soaking wet. Somebody had filled my locker up to the air vents with water. That day I had to call home to have dry clothing sent up to school.

I didn't like to call home during the day because I knew each time the phone rang my mom would worry that it was the call she dreaded—the call informing her that her son had been killed. We had never openly discussed it, but I knew that my mom would pick up the phone each time it rang before it completed one full ring. She was that anxious about what might happen to me.

Although I did not learn about it until years later, my mom had received a call one school day from a person who sounded very official and said that I had been savagely beaten and would probably not live for another half hour. Evidently he gave her gory details that made the scene in her mind vivid and devastatingly frightening. He described how I had been smashed on the head with tire irons, how I had bled profusely, and how he could see broken bones protruding from my arms. She had rushed up to Central High, distraught and filled with anxiety, only to find that I was sitting in class without a scratch.

The principal, who helped her calm down a bit, had taken her to my classroom and allowed her to peek inside to see that I was okay, that nothing had actually happened. But the psychological damage had been done.

My mom kept that information to herself because she didn't want me to worry about her. When she did tell me the story, twenty years later, after we had moved to California, I was overwhelmed. I felt responsible for her pain and anguish. She said she knew I would feel that way and that was the reason she had waited to tell me. With a mother's intuition, she had rightly figured that adding this concern for her might make it too difficult for me to continue at Central.

I withheld information from her as well. While I could not conceal scratches or abrasions, I did keep much of what happened to me each day away from her. She burned my hate mail, and I lied about the pain I felt each day. We tried hard to shield each other.

The level of stress all nine of us felt that year was unbelievable. And the lessons we learned about stress are imprinted indelibly upon each one of our brains. We remember well the terror of myriad stressful situations as well as the power of threat to induce stress. We felt the terror in our bones and imagined unspeakable horror as we stared into the twisted, contorted faces of students who gave every indication that they intended to do to us whatever it took to force us out of Central High.

Each time my books were torn from my grasp and summarily destroyed as I stood in the hallway and watched, I felt powerful fear and anxiety. Each time I chose to run away from threatening situations as they developed around me, each time I was surprised by a hard blow from behind, each time I dodged the sharp-edged objects thrown toward me, I had to conjure up thoughts that helped to keep my fear in check. I often thought of lines from William Earnest Henley's "Invictus":

> In the fell clutch of circumstance
> I have not winced nor cried aloud
> Under the bludgeonings of chance
> My head is bloody but unbowed.

That slowed my heartbeat and gave me a measure of control over sphincters that sought immediate release. I must have sweated buckets of perspiration that year in one stressful situation after another.

Sitting in my English class that year was an ongoing exercise in stress management. The tall, thin, severe-faced teacher communicated clearly that she was not happy about my presence in her class. The students who shared her attitude seized every possible opportunity to devise some scheme to cause me grief. This sometimes caused me to question my own sanity about being there. It was not at all unusual for things to be thrown at me during class sessions—and for the teacher to claim she had no knowledge of any of it. Just maintaining the high level of vigilance I needed to avoid serious injury was extremely stressful. To have a hostile teacher on top of it was almost too much.

On one day, this English teacher asked me: "Why do you want to go to *our* school, why don't you go back to your own school?" I had no ready response. What do you say to such idiocy? How could a qualified educator come to the conclusion that public school ownership could be divided up among racial groups? I simply smiled and walked away. I have since learned that smiling and walking away is my usual response to idiocy wherever I find it.

12

The Penknife and the Switchblade

My fear during the time I spent at Central was much greater than I could ever have imagined. It was the kind of gut-wrenching fear that comes with a sense of powerlessness. I knew I had the option of saying, "I don't want to go back up there another day." And that option called out to me at times in ways that were hard to resist. On those days when life at school had demanded more of me than I thought I had to give, saying "no more" had a sweet appeal.

During the long Thanksgiving holiday weekend, I visited my sister, Juereta, at Oakwood College in Huntsville, Alabama. My parents decided it would be good for me to get away from Little Rock, and Reta agreed to stay at school so we could be together. That proved to be a very therapeutic time for me. I was able to relax and release a lot of the tension that had built up during the preceding weeks.

But as the Thanksgiving weekend came to a close, it was hard to think of going back to Central and putting myself through all of that chaos. But in the end, I realized that it was not just about me and my need for comfort and personal safety. It was about the need for change, real change in a social system more than demeaning to black Americans.

At age fifteen, my thinking was of course not fully developed, but even then I knew that what the nine of us were doing included accepting fear and still saying "yes, I will return." Fear will go with you wherever you go, but it will not prevent your accomplishing anything you want if you want that thing badly enough. Yes, I was afraid, but something inside me wanted to return to Central High. And so return I did.

I felt I had to make this decision to return because there were so many people who were willing to offer help and support for our efforts. I had gotten letters from people all over the United States and from people in other countries pledging to support me with their prayers. Plus I knew that many people had already given their lives to advance this very same cause. I felt that dropping out would have been tantamount to spitting on the graves of those folk. So following my brief respite at Oakwood College, I returned to Central. I learned to use the weekends during the remaining school year as mini-breaks from the violence at Central. But Monday mornings still presented a Herculean challenge.

Conventional wisdom holds that stress can kill you if it is allowed free rein in your life. Much scientific data has shown the relationship between stress-producing situations and the subsequent response of the body's various systems. I recall reading a recent report wherein the authors noted that most of the heart attacks suffered by American males occur on Monday mornings, just before time to report to work. The implication is that the anticipation of confronting overwhelming responsibilities and duties is enough to induce a heart attack. This makes sense to me.

When I think about the stressful situations that awaited the nine of us each morning at Central High School, I understand from a very personal perspective what stress can do to the body and mind. The lessons we learned about stress are imprinted indelibly upon each of our brains; we remember well the terror we felt in our bones. We imagined horrific violence as we stared into the hate-filled faces of students who meant to force us out of Central High.

Stress has a way of interfering with all parts of a person: the physical, the psychological, the social, the mental, and the spiritual.

The demands placed on the body and the mind are extraordinary in the wake of stressful events. There is no adequate preparation for the physiological changes that occur so rapidly. Oh, you can breathe deeply and recite mantras if you wish, but I tell you truthfully, stress is scary stuff! It throws you off balance enough so that planned responses, unless they are automatic and can function without conscious input, are of no use whatsoever.

I don't remember ever thinking about exactly how I was going to respond to the stress of being in Central High. My reactions and responses were pretty much off the cuff—mostly about getting myself to some place of relative safety, out of the line of fire, so to speak, about paying attention to the immediate surroundings, gauging the potential for violence, and staying far away from such areas as much as possible. This was not always possible; I was faced many times with terrifying situations.

I remember when one of the soldiers in the hallway once pulled me aside and said, "Don't leave the building by that door; there's a bunch of boys waiting for you." I was relieved to have the information, but my anxiety was heightened as thoughts raced through my mind: *What if there are other groups? And where are they? Will they be able to hide so the soldiers can't see them?*

I hurriedly found another exit that seemed to offer safe passage out of the building. In this case it was the threat of violence, not an actual attack. But a threat is one of the most horrendous tools of oppression that we know about. The mind simply takes in the threatened action and multiplies its size and weight until it looms much larger than it might ever be in reality. As hostile students would whisper what they intended to do, my entire being would respond, regardless of the likelihood of the threatened action or their ability to pull it off. I always assumed the worst. How could I not? Certainly I had seen attempts by some of them to inflict great pain and injury on us, and I had been hit often enough, hard enough, to know that there was serious intent here. A casual remark alluding to some proposed assault was enough to start my mind's enlarging the thing and creating stress in direct proportion to my notions about what would actually take place if and when the threat were made real.

Nothing had changed at Central while I was away at Oakwood. Tuley was still there, and so were all the others who harbored the same degree of hatred toward black people as he did. One day shortly after the Thanksgiving holiday break, I walked into my homeroom with my radar on full alert for anything that seemed out of the ordinary. It would have been unusual if there had been nothing out of the ordinary.

A ray of sunlight glanced off the seat of my desk, and I saw that one of my classmates had emptied a bottle of glue for me to sit in. Without a word or sign of recognition, I quickly moved my desk out and replaced it with the one in front of my place in line. Then I put my desk in the vacated space and sat down to wait for the kid who sat in front of me. When he came in, nobody said anything because nobody "knew" anything. He was outraged when he sat in the glue and demanded that the person responsible be punished. But nobody knew anything, so nobody could say anything.

Algebra class was a haven for me. The teacher, Mrs. Helen Conrad, let it be known from the first day I was in class that she would not tolerate any nonsense from anyone who opposed my presence. She was emphatic about it and the class responded accordingly. It was in this algebra class that I met Robin Woods, a white student who shared her textbook with me. Since my books and other school supplies were routinely destroyed by fellow students, I would come to class often without a book or any supplies. Robin simply pulled her desk next to mine one day and we shared her book. This act did not win her friends or favor. Her kindness was interpreted as a violation of the social code that outlawed any contact between black students and white students, especially black males and white females. You might say that Robin's action gave merit to the fear held by many white people that we black students had one thought in mind, to sexually captivate the white students.

White students who befriended any of the nine of us were labeled "nigger lovers" and harassed by those who wanted to preserve the old social order. Robin had had the fortunate experience of growing up in a home with parents who taught her to treat all people as equals. And they truly meant what they said. Some kids grow up in homes where they hear the rhetoric of acceptance and inclusion. But often, in such homes, when one of the hated "others" is brought home, there is a quick conference in the kitchen where the real message is delivered: "Don't you ever bring such a person into our house again!" Robin's home was unusual in that there was consistency between word and deed. But none of this mattered to those who felt she had overstepped the line. Robin was labeled a "nigger lover" and chased home the day she shared her book with me.

I had not seen or talked to Robin for many years until 1994 when the two of us were invited to appear on the *Oprah Winfrey Show* along with six other members of the Little Rock Nine. The program assistants had asked me if there were any white kids at Central who were friendly to us, and I mentioned Robin's name immediately. *Oprah Show* representatives called me later to say that they could not find Robin and we would proceed without her on the show. What I did not know at the time was that they had located her and intended to surprise me on the show by having Robin appear at some point in the program. It worked out in just that fashion, and I was truly surprised, and delighted, to have a reunion with one of the few students at Central who had gone out of her way to make me feel accepted there.

I did not have the same kind of allies in other classes during that year. My Spanish teacher, Mrs. Bell, was in her last year before retiring and simply did not have the energy to cope with the madness taking place around her. In her class I had one of my more bizarre encounters with another student. One day the student sitting across from me on the right stood his Spanish textbook up on end as a shield to hide what he was doing from the teacher. He unfolded a penknife, pointed the blade toward me, and glared. The look on his face said, "I'm going to cut out your liver."

Why he chose that particular day I do not know, but it was an unlucky day for him. One of my friends from Horace Mann had been urging me for several weeks to take his switchblade knife and carry it with me while I was in school. "Come on, Robbie, just take it. I'll feel bad if you get in trouble over at Central and I haven't done anything to help you. Just put it in your pocket; it'll make me feel better." I had declined repeatedly saying that carrying a knife would be a violation of the nonviolence stance we had adopted. But just the day before, I had said "yes," I would take the knife. My friend was visibly relieved, and I justified taking it because of his obvious satisfaction.

The school board, in deference to the fears expressed by white citizens in Little Rock that we would become socially (read *sexually*) involved with white students, had required the nine of us to sign an affidavit that we would not engage in any extracurricular activities at Central, so we hung out with our former Horace Mann schoolmates. We went to dances and parties at Mann, and continued to see our friends socially and at church. They were part of a significant group of people who gave us unqualified support and encouragement. My friend was just one of many who wanted to protect us, and he gave me the knife as a token of his concern.

I don't know exactly why I let my friend talk me into taking the knife to school, but I happened to have it in my pocket that day in Spanish class. Calmly, as if this were the most natural thing in the world, I put my textbook on end the same as the kid sitting across from me and pulled the switchblade out of my pocket. Returning his glare, I flicked the switch. The menacing blade popped out, pointing in his direction. The blade on my knife was longer than his entire knife, and I tried to make the look on my face say, "My liver is now under protection." This standoff lasted for a minute or so until he folded up his penknife and put it away. I did the same with the switchblade.

I had no other occasion to show my friend's switchblade off, and perhaps that student's report to his friends saved me from other potentially dangerous encounters. I often wondered, though, what would have happened if he had reported me to the principal. I am certain that would have set the stereotypes flying and I would most certainly have been expelled from school.

If you have seen or will see *The Ernie Green Story*, a movie made by Disney, you will recognize this scene. In the movie, Ernie is the knife-wielding black student, but in truth, this happened to me. I agreed to allow Disney to use the story as a way of sharing with the viewers what life inside the school was really like for all of us.

My English and history classes were taught by teachers who probably would have preferred that the whole desegregation experiment be abandoned and the sooner the better. In those classrooms I had to be especially alert and on guard because I could not count on the teachers to look out for me. Flying can openers or paper clips shot from rubber bands or thumb tacks on my desk seat did not elicit any warnings or reprimands from these two stalwart educators. Instead I was told to refrain from whining and, besides, they didn't see anything anyway. Whenever possible, I would request permission to go to the library to do in-class assignments. This provided some relief, although the librarian was a stickler about the rules, which did not permit doing in-class assignments in the library. I had to use all of my creative abilities to come up with reasons why I should be allowed to spend time in the library.

The agreement the school officials forced us to sign meant that we would not be involved in sports, dances, choral groups, drama clubs, school band, debate teams, language clubs, or any other activity that would entail social interaction. We were told that for reasons of safety we should avoid such things. We knew of course that this was a way of mollifying those parents and other concerned white citizens who felt our primary goal in coming to Central was to develop romantic and sexual attachments to white students. One of the many printed cards passed around the campus that year showed a silhouette of a black male and a white female figure hand-in-hand. No text or caption, just the visual message that seemed to need no further explanation.

We led very isolated lives at Central that 1957-58 school year. But our lack of social interaction was made up for by our continued participation in extracurricular school activities at Horace Mann. The feeling of acceptance with the students at Mann helped tremendously. We could and did attend school functions with our former classmates and felt less like social outcasts as a result. Some students at Mann were resentful because they thought the nine of us might be developing attitudes of superiority now that we were in the "white" school. A few times they chose to say so, and there were some ugly moments. At a party one Saturday night somebody yelled across the room to ask me how to spell a word, and I yelled back the correct spelling. This seemed to infuriate one of the partygoers, who began to badger me about what he sensed to be my "know-it-all" attitude since I was now mingling with whites. What he didn't know was that my ability to spell came from countless hours of reading the dictionary and had nothing to do with my being at Central or hanging out with white students. This student probably had some issues about his own ability to compete in a world of white people.

I left the party early that night because I didn't feel up to explaining my point of view. Even with occasional outbursts like that one, getting together with our friends from Mann helped us a lot to release the tensions that built up as we endured our days at Central High.

13

THE EMOTIONAL PRICE OF NON-VIOLENCE

The 101st were on campus for about five weeks during the first part of the school year. They were then replaced by the newly federalized Arkansas National Guardsmen who remained at school for the rest of the academic year. On the surface there was no real difference between the groups of soldiers, and it would have been hard for the casual observer to tell which group was present. They were all soldiers and as such were accustomed to obeying orders from commanding officers.

The Arkansas troops protected us, albeit with not as much vigor as the members of the 101st. I am certain there was some reluctance on their part to fully defend us simply because they were Southern white people, some of whom harbored the same negative ideas about black people as some of their civilian counterparts. But, that said, the soldiers went about their task of protecting us with as much military discipline as they could muster.

After the year-end holidays, things changed in a way that led to an increase in the amount of violence we had to endure. One of our group of nine, Minnijean Brown, was no longer enrolled at Central after mid-February. The daily hostilities had escalated to a point beyond Minnijean's ability or desire to use nonviolence in response. The simple truth is that we were all approaching that same point! Several white students had made it their business to aggravate

Minnijean by calling her names and pushing her around in the halls with even more intensity than ever before. Rumor had it that many white students were outraged that Minnijean seemed to walk around the school "as if she belonged there." There had been a scuffle or two between Minnijean and some of her tormentors, and the situation appeared to be escalating. Then one day in the school cafeteria, faced with an especially nasty kid who pushed his chair back when Minnijean attempted to pass his table, things came to a boiling point. As she stood there looking at this kid with his attitude of defiance, Minnijean simply dumped her bowl of chili onto his head. After a brief period of absolute silence, the cafeteria serving staff, the vast majority of whom were black females, burst into spontaneous applause.

This cheerleading notwithstanding, Minnijean was expelled from school. Her departure encouraged the troublemakers among the white students who immediately began to chant "One down, eight to go!" In fact, printed cards with that same rallying cry were distributed all over the school. The students did indeed step up their attacks on the other eight of us sensing that perhaps we too would give in to the impulse to strike back in retaliation. We simply rededicated ourselves to nonviolence and managed to restrain ourselves in the face of the increased pressures.

The school officials could not—nor did they try to—make a rational case for kicking Minnijean out of school. They argued that if any of us fought back, it would simply make things too difficult to manage and it would be more dangerous for us. We were proud of Minnijean for doing what we all wanted so badly to do. We felt sorry that she would not be with us for the remainder of the term. Some years later we learned from Minnijean that she had felt at the time that she had let us down, but we rushed to assure her that was not the case. She had acted as our proxy in giving back a small measure of what we had to endure.

I felt personally that I had let Minnijean down by not defending her against a vicious attack by one of the white male students. One afternoon as we waited outside for transportation home from school, a white male student ran up behind Minnijean and kicked her hard in the rear. I was standing next to her when it happened and could have retaliated since the kid did not attempt to leave. He just glowered as if daring me to do something. But I did nothing. I did not sleep well that night and tried to rationalize my behavior by reminding myself of our decision to respond with nonviolence. For a long time after that incident I berated myself for being cowardly and for not standing up in defense of black womanhood.

I remember another occasion when I was sitting in the back row of seats in the school auditorium awaiting the start of a student assembly. As I sat there, a white male student kicked the back of my chair. The very thin, contoured wooden back of the seat did little to soften the blow. The blow was sudden, unexpected, and shock registered on my face as I turned to face my attacker. The look on his face was unmistakable. The message was clear: *I don't like you, nigger, and I want to hurt you.* For me it was a defining moment. There was little if any chance that meaningful connection could be made with my attacker. The distance between us was too great to be spanned. I remember thinking as I looked at him that his choice was irreversible. He was invested in causing me grief, and no amount of dialogue would persuade him to think differently.

I despaired about this realization; I knew even then that the only way to change the situation was through some kind of honest dialogue. Even if he had been willing to start the conversation with "Terry Roberts, I hate you because you're black," we could have begun to dismantle the wall of separation between us. But as it was, we had no opportunity to move. It took much effort on my part to remain stoic and continue in this uncertain experiment in desegregation.

That's one thing about the Central High experience I wish could have been different: I wish we could have sat and talked about our strong feelings and resentments. That's still the only way I know how to resolve things. Years earlier my mom had taught all of us kids not to fight with each other. She had explained that while we were animals, we were human animals with brains and minds that allowed us to choose responses other than violence when disputes arose. I believed her then, and I believe today that this makes much more sense than fighting.

At the end of the school year we were a battered crew, both physically and psychologically. Somehow we had come through the ordeal more or less intact, albeit with scars as proof of our engagement with the forces of opposition. One question people often ask me is, "How did you manage to stay focused on schoolwork with all that was going on around you?" The short answer is that we were all good students and it was just a matter of adjustment, making the necessary shifts to screen out the distractions. A more complete answer, however, would require that each one of us provide a detailed description of all the various methods we used to keep our minds on academics. Looking back on this situation from my vantage point as a psychologist, I can say without doubt that we would have benefited from some kind of professional clinical intervention. As far as I know, such a thing was never proposed at the time, and our own awareness of such possibilities was extremely limited. I do know that if we had made use of some kind of therapeutic assistance, we would have been better able to handle the emotional residue that has plagued many of us over the years.

In my own case, since I had determined as far back as first grade to become the "executive in charge of my own education," it was merely an opportunity to make an executive decision that took into account the daily threats and the actual violence we had to endure. Any good executive will tell you the goal is always much more relevant than the potential barriers to achieving that goal. At Central I used my thinking to gain a measure of control in the face of seemingly out-of-control situations. I prided myself on my ability to think quickly and to anticipate the development of dangerous situations. If I saw the possibility of danger in the way a group of students began to behave, I would turn around and go rapidly in the other direction. This heightened awareness helps explain how I was also able to focus on schoolwork. Since I knew my time for actual attention to school assignments would be limited, I made full use of the time available. In other words, rather than fret about not having enough time or worry about what might happen next, I directed my attention to school lessons in any available space.

My end-of-year report demonstrates the success of my methods during the year. I finished with two A's and two B's, and although I could very well have made a case that I deserved four A's, I chose not to confront the issue. Some battles are not worth the effort.

In truth, I think my English teacher must have initially given me an F. I say this because the woman most surely hated me, as she demonstrated by the way she looked at me each time I walked into her class. She could twist her face into the most grotesque mask of hatred you could imagine. And, if you recall, she was the teacher who had asked me why I wanted to go to their school, the school for white students, since I had a school of my own. At any rate, my theory is that she gave me the F but had a twinge of conscience overnight, snuck into school early the next morning, and changed the grade. And would you believe it, wonder of wonders, I received an A in English. Now there is absolutely no way to explain that A. But I must admit that I am tempted to consider the notion that my obvious genius was just too difficult to ignore.

Not only would it have been good to sit and talk with the students, but also with the teachers at Central. Perhaps out of that dialogue, those teachers with more liberal attitudes could have influenced their colleagues to rethink their positions. The more I consider this possibility, the more I am motivated to try to achieve such results wherever I am.

14

Lessons from the Barbershop and Lawn-Mowing Clients

For a long time before I had the opportunity to go to Central I had reasoned that either I had to change Little Rock in some way or live somewhere else. It made no sense to me that discrimination was allowed by law and custom, and that human energy was expended in such ludicrous ways to maintain a system that maimed everybody's spirit.

When I was about ten years old, I was riding in the back seat of a station wagon with my mom and her catering partner, Lois Jordan. The two of them cooked and served more meals than I can count. I was often pressed into service as a general helper, and I was with them when this episode occurred. That day Lois was driving us to a catering assignment. As we approached a downtown intersection I noticed a traffic cop directing cars and pedestrians. Suddenly, and for no apparent reason, he ran over to the car and began banging on the left front fender with his nightstick. He yelled to Lois, "You better pay attention to me!" Then he motioned for us to continue through the intersection. Neither Lois nor my mom said a word. My heart was racing and adrenaline was flowing nonstop, but I knew better than to ask questions. It was one of those times when black adults knew that what had happened was not justifiable, but they were not allowed to complain. The white cop had the right to dent Lois's fender and treat us with disrespect in the process. Our rights were unclear at best.

In my ten-year-old mind this had to change—or I had to leave.
I had no idea where I might wind up, but the prospect of staying in
Little Rock under these conditions was too depressing for me to
consider what my next stop would be. Of course, in reality, I had very
little to say about where I would live at that age, but the thoughts were
comforting.

For some people, the continuing lesson from Little Rock about
race and racism is that change can happen, over time, and slowly. But
time itself is neutral, and without concentrated, sustained effort by
human beings, change will not occur. Even in the face of the
oppressive legal conditions governing life in Little Rock before the
Brown decision in 1954, black citizens had pressed forward in the legal
arenas seeking to overturn the onerous laws and regulations that
interfered with their efforts to participate fully in the socioeconomic
and political life of the city.

For example, my parents had to pay a poll tax in order to qualify
as voters in Little Rock. The poll tax was one of the many ways used
to thwart black citizens who wanted to help determine political
outcomes. By imposing this financial burden on those who could least
afford it, the members of the white power structure ensured that
control of the political process would remain firmly in their hands. My
parents and many other black people in like circumstances could not
vote because they lacked the necessary funds to pay the poll tax. The
poll tax was finally eliminated by a concentrated, focused action on
the part of concerned black and white people. It was *not* eliminated by
the passage of time.

One of the many amazing things about life in the American
South during this era was the seeming ease with which people
interacted across racial lines as long as there seemed to be mutual
acceptance of the lines of social demarcation. Expressions of
friendship from both sides of the racial divide were common if there
were no challenges to the status quo. And of course there were the

"good" white people defined by their relative lack of overt bias in dealing with the black people who cooked their food, cleaned their houses, chauffeured them around, and cared for their children. Their black employees merited the label "good nigras." Neither black people nor white people would think of violating the rules of proper social etiquette by speaking openly with each other about such things, but the rules and names existed and were spoken about freely by both blacks and whites.

Home, school, and community were virtually one-race settings for me. Sitting in the all-black barbershop waiting my turn for a haircut was one of the most fascinating adventures of my young life. It was here that older black men took it upon themselves to give us boys the benefit of their best thinking about the whole of life. They did it generally to the group most of the time, but it was not uncommon to find yourself singled out for instruction about some aspect of your apparel, attitude, or ambition. I remember once when a barber gave me a nickel and said I could play any song on the jukebox that I wanted. After I made my selection, the entire assemblage began to critique my choice in terms of what my selection said about my character and my level of music appreciation. I had chosen "Lawdy Miss Clawdy," a blues number by Lloyd Price that was a popular favorite. The lyrics went, "Well, lawdy, lawdy, lawdy, Miss Clawdy; girl you sho' look good to me. Please don't excite me, baby, I know it can't be me." The consensus in the barbershop was that I should not be so eager to listen to that "gut-bucket music."

There was no way to anticipate what the tenor of remarks might be in these situations; you simply absorbed all of it without complaint. I was expected to pay attention to these words of wisdom, and I did. To me these men were just members of my extended family taking it upon themselves to file away the rough edges of my character. And though at times their language was gruff and the admonitions crudely put, I knew they had my best interests at heart.

In the barbershop as I waited for my turn in the chair, I learned which white people were the "good" ones and how to tell if a given white person qualified for the label. Even though nobody ever said as much to me about it, I sensed that this sharing of information was considered essential for survival.

The "bad nigger" was discussed in those barbershop conversations as well. It seemed to me that this character scared both black folks and white folks. He challenged anybody and everybody because the threat he represented could destroy the delicate balance needed to maintain the racist status quo.

I have often thought that the people who fit the definition of "bad nigger" were those who found racism so onerous they simply could not accept their own passive participation in a system designed to maintain white supremacy. The nine of us, in the eyes of many white people in Little Rock, were indeed "bad niggers." In fact, there were rumors suggesting that we had been imported from Northern cities, probably New York or Chicago, especially to participate in the desegregation of Central. In the minds of Southern racists, there was no way to compute the fact that homegrown "nigras" would deliberately choose to confront—and try to change—the social system that had been in place for so long.

In the year prior to my going to Central, I had developed a small business that included mowing lawns and raking leaves. The majority of my customers were white. As long as I presented myself as one who would work hard and stay within the bounds of socially prescribed behavior, I could look forward to having as much work as possible. When it became common knowledge that I was one of the Nine, most of the whites I had worked for canceled my services. The question from most of those who talked to me was, "Why do you want to go to a white school?" In fact, Little Rock prided itself on having the "finest school for Negroes in all the South." This was in reference to Dunbar High School, which was for a very long time the only high school for black people in Little Rock. After 1955, Dunbar was used only as a junior high school since the new Horace Mann High School had opened.

One woman in particular, Mrs. Montgomery, expressed a feeling of disappointment that I would act in what she considered to be such an uncharacteristic way. My mom had worked as a maid and cook for her for many years, and she had been a fairly generous customer for me. But my choice to attend Central was too much for her to bear. I was no longer acceptable. She could not, in good conscience, hire a black person who harbored thoughts of being equal to her and her kind.

She must have been somewhat aware of the possibility of my choosing to be part of the nine students. Just a year or so before, my Uncle Leady, returning from a stint in the Korean War, had dropped by to visit her and refused to enter her home by the back door as was the usual custom. He had insisted that he be allowed to enter the front door, and she had agreed. Perhaps she had been so stunned by his request that she did not have time to argue with him. He was my mom's younger brother and was well known to the Montgomery family. He reasoned that if he had to fight to protect them, white people could, and should, treat him with basic respect.

My next-door neighbor, a black woman who worked in the cafeteria at Central, was very disturbed about my being involved in the desegregation efforts because she thought her job was in jeopardy. She confronted me one day and asked the same question I had gotten from some of my white customers: "Why do you want to go to that school? You and the others are just messing things up!" I felt bad that she was so upset, but I was confused about her logic. It was not us messing things up—things had been "messed up" for years—we were simply trying to straighten things out.

Fortunately, for me, she was a minority of one. I am certain there were others like her, but none of them expressed their feelings or thoughts openly to me. But even as I felt a bit perturbed that she would take such a position, I think I understood her fears about losing her job.

Apart from the constant harassment at school, most of the criticism I received that year came in the form of hate mail and menacing telephone calls. My mom burned most of the mail, and she tried to screen all the calls. But I managed to hang on to some of the mail. It's incredible to think that people from all over the United States took time to put in writing their racist ideas and thoughts. One enigmatic telegram I am still trying to figure out read: "We can never forget what you did here." It was signed, "A White Lady." The most positive spin would be that she liked what happened and would cherish the memory, but there are other obvious possibilities.

One of the longest letters I received came from Los Angeles, California, and was scrawled in pencil on several sheets of notebook paper. The author seemed to be outraged by the fact that the nine of us would dare challenge such a perfectly fine system of racial segregation since it was in keeping with God's admonition to keep the races separate.

15

UNEXPECTED MOVE TO LOS ANGELES

The 1957-58 school year had been filled with fear and anxiety for me. And it ended with no real sense of resolution about the continued desegregation effort in Little Rock. Even so, I was all set to return the following year as a high school senior. In spite of the fact that we had been so beaten down, both physically and psychologically, I was ready to go back and face the hatred and hostilities most surely awaiting us. During the school year when we were dealing with it all, and even as I thought many times about quitting, about giving up and going back to Horace Mann, I was also building a solid resolve to stay and continue my part in the fight for equality. It's hard to say what enabled me to sustain this kind of thinking, but I believe it was rooted in my growing awareness that white people needed to understand that we black people and those who supported us were tired of the indignities heaped upon us by the system of racial separation. The more I witnessed events around me in Little Rock—and all over the United States—the clearer it became that backing down now was simply not an option.

I hoped my senior year would end much as it had for Ernie Green, the lone senior in our group of nine. He had marched across the stage to muted applause, but he had accomplished his goal of obtaining his high school diploma. I assumed I would march across the stage set up on the Central High athletic field and receive my diploma without fanfare as well. I certainly did not expect that things would have changed for the better over the short period of time it would take me to graduate and that I might enjoy the kind of raucous applause usually heard at high school graduations all over America. After all, it had been necessary to have a strong military presence at Ernie's graduation, and the other seven of us (Minnijean was in New York) had not been allowed to attend the ceremony out of concern for our safety and well-being. No, things would not have changed drastically, but still I was ready and determined to return.

During the summer of 1958 the nine of us were once again "on display." We were invited to appear on programs around the country sponsored by civic and social organizations of every stripe. I remember participating in a parade in Washington, D.C., where the nine of us rode on a float sitting at school desks. We were interviewed, photographed, profiled in publications, and otherwise presented to the public as the famous "Little Rock Nine." Even though we tolerated it, none of us were that keen about doing any of it. Fortunately, Ernie Green and I went to New York to work at summer jobs in the garment industry and missed a lot of those "opportunities."

Ernie and I became card-carrying members of the International Ladies' Garment Workers' Union and lived and worked in New York until August. Ernie worked in the union office and I worked as a shipping clerk in the warehouse at Diana Stores. We lived in a rooming house in Queens and took the subway into Manhattan each weekday morning.

Our landlady was Mrs. Brown, who had come to New York from her homeland of Jamaica. She gave us a lot of good advice about how to survive in the "big city." In fact, it was Mrs. Brown who gave us insight into the nightlife in New York. One Friday we rushed home from work because Mrs. Brown had invited us to a party at one of her friends' homes in Harlem. We got ready to go, only to learn that we would not be leaving until about 11 p.m. That was news to us. As it turned out, when we arrived at the party some time after midnight, we were early! The party lasted until 8 o'clock Saturday morning, and we discovered that this was the ordinary New York way of life.

While we were in New York we spent a lot of time at the home of Drs. Kenneth and Mamie Clark, black psychologists whose work with black children and their preferences for white dolls had been used to support the *Brown* decision. The Clarks lived in Hastings-on-the-Hudson, a few miles up the Hudson River from the city. They had offered Minnijean a place to live when she was expelled from Central. Ernie and I would often visit the Clarks to see Minnijean.

The three of us, along with the Clarks' teenaged daughter, Kate, explored Manhattan together. We had a great time taking in all the lights and noise of New York and getting to know each other in less turbulent surroundings. I was so fascinated by New York that I wanted to stay there to finish high school, but my parents would not hear of it. So I returned to Little Rock expecting to go back to Central.

How wrong I was. Governor Faubus decided to use his authority to close all of Little Rock's high schools for the entire academic year 1958-59. His action was consistent with the actions of other Southern governors in their adoption of "massive resistance" policies. In the name of "segregation forever," he was willing to sacrifice the education of all of Little Rock's high school students, black and white alike. What he may not have known, or even cared about, was that this action would result in many students, both black and white, giving up any educational ambitions. I might add here that his was not the most egregious use of this tactic; schools in Prince Edward County in Virginia were closed for four consecutive years for the same reason.

With the schools closed, I was forced to leave Little Rock. I didn't want to miss an entire year of school, and my family didn't have the money to send me to a private school. So I moved to Los Angeles to live with my aunt and uncle, Zenobia and Clinton Hill. This allowed me to continue school without interruption, and I graduated in 1959 from Los Angeles High School.

The other members of the Little Rock Nine who had been juniors in the school year 1957-58 also found creative ways to complete their high school education. Melba, Minnijean, Elizabeth, and I graduated from schools outside Little Rock, and Thelma Mothershed actually obtained a high school diploma from Central by having credits transferred from Southern Illinois University.

My own sister Beverly, however, spent the year at home helping to take care of our younger siblings. And while some other black students also were able to move to other states or to afford private schools closer to home, many of my friends and others I knew about did not fare as well. They lost the momentum they needed to carry them through the year of unstructured activity. Too many wound up working in dead-end jobs, falling into criminal activity, giving themselves up to drugs, fathering or bearing children, and missing out on gaining high school diplomas. Many of them, as a result, made themselves ineligible for good job opportunities. This often relegated them to lives lived below the poverty line.

Whether the governor ever thought about these consequences, or whether he even cared, remains a mystery to me. What is clear is that he was willing to behave in this way because of his unbending allegiance to the myth of white supremacy.

The Little Rock schools were re-opened for the school year 1959-60, and two of our group of nine, Carlotta Walls and Jefferson Thomas, returned as seniors. They had been sophomores during the initial year of integration and had completed their junior year at other schools. They were joined by a few other black students. The entire group of them had to contend with the hostilities without the support of the army.

In many ways their experience during that year—and the experience of the black students who followed during the decade of the sixties—was harder because they had to cope with the pressures without the military presence that had been provided for the nine of us. I have talked to several of the black students who were enrolled in

Central during that time period, and their experiences of overt hostility from teachers and students are very similar to my own. The governor would probably say this was because the people were not ready for integration and that we would simply have to let time pass until people were ready.

I had an opportunity to confront the governor a few years later. In fact, on two separate occasions, I charged him with malfeasance and described his actions as racist and felonious. In 1973, we appeared together on ABC's *Good Morning America* show; and we met again in Abilene, Kansas, in 1987, where we took part in an oral history project at the Eisenhower Presidential Library. Both times he refused to consider my point of view and defended his actions by saying that if he had not made the decisions he made in Little Rock in 1957, he would have been voted out of office and we would have had to contend with someone worse than he was. Knowing that he considered himself a political moderate, I took his statement to mean that another governor would likely have been more overtly racist. It is hard to imagine, however, that the situation could have been more dangerous for us.

In view of the governor's decision to close all of the Little Rock public high schools, it wasn't difficult for me to decide to leave Little Rock to finish high school in Los Angeles. I left with a feeling of relief that I would not have to face daily aggression at school and with a feeling of optimism about the future. Life in Los Angeles was different from life in Little Rock in many ways. But there, too, black people were facing an uphill struggle in their quest for equality. Even so, my optimism remained vibrant and strong. The war was not over, but how hard would it be with the palm trees and sunny days of California?

***

My youthful optimism would be challenged often over the years, and I learned many painful lessons about life in the United States. I remember once, when I was apartment hunting in the West Adams district of Los Angeles, a white landlord cursed at me and ordered me off his property. Evidently his note inviting prospective tenants to step inside the foyer was meant for whites only. By this time I was married and the father of two daughters. Now I not only had to contend with racism directed toward me, but I had the responsibility of guiding my new family through the roiling waters of racial hatred.

16

THOSE WHO WOULD RE-WRITE HISTORY

I entered UCLA as a freshman and eventually earned a bachelor's degree from California State University at Los Angeles. I returned to UCLA for a master's degree in social welfare, and my growing fascination with the ways people responded to life's challenges led me to complete work for a doctoral degree at Southern Illinois University at Carbondale. Today, as a practicing psychologist, I have continued to work toward the elimination of racism by teaching others how to cope with difference. I do this in university classrooms, workshops, and in my private practice. And I speak often to groups of people who have questions about and interest in the desegregation of Central High School.

I have returned to Little Rock on several occasions, some of which have marked the passage of time since our initial desegregation efforts in 1957. In 1987 the nine of us returned to mark the passage of thirty years and to review the progress toward real change for the better. During this visit I had an opportunity to meet the governor of Arkansas, William Jefferson (Bill) Clinton. My impression of Governor Clinton was that he was a man who believed strongly in this country's ability—and will—to confront and resolve issues that had bedeviled us for many years.

The nine of us spent an evening at the Governor's Mansion talking long into the night with Bill and Hillary Clinton about what might be done about racial discrimination, health care reform, education, employment, and other concerns. I remember thinking that Bill Clinton could be president, especially if he continued to pursue resolution of all the things we talked about that night at the Governor's Mansion. I was not surprised at all when he was selected by the Democratic Party to be their nominee for president in 1992.

We assembled again in 1997 in Little Rock to spend time reviewing all that had transpired during the past forty years. Many in Little Rock and in other places in the nation like to point out that positive changes have occurred since the days when segregation was legal and constitutional. Yet they seem reluctant to address the residual elements of years of segregation and discrimination which still exist. During both the 30th and the 40th anniversary events planned in Little Rock, speakers at various programs talked about celebrating the positive changes and seeking reconciliation. They urged us to get on with our new life which, by their reckoning, was devoid of the most onerous aspects of discrimination.

But black family income continues to fall disproportionately below the poverty line. And the preponderance of black males populating our prisons is unconscionable. These facts should alarm us. We should not be deluded that we have reached some kind of racial equality in our culture. We must not entertain the wishful thinking that racism is a thing of the past. These and many other indicators reveal the inconvenient but unavoidable truth: the work our courageous ancestors began, and which we risked our lives to continue, is far from over.

I reminded those to whom I spoke that it was not yet time for celebration, that reconciliation was possible only if there had been some meaningful connection in the past that was now broken and in need of repair. In fact, in 1997 I wrote an editorial piece for the *Arkansas Democrat-Gazette* in which I pointed out that it was misleading to talk about reconciliation since we had not ever established any kind of fruitful connection in the past. I quote from my own writing:

> When I consider that the battle rages still in 1997, I realize that I have no time for celebration. Time for reflection, yes. Time for remembering the past so the future can be better informed, yes. But as Little Rock's schools remain under federal orders to desegregate, as affirmative action programs are being dismantled across the country, as statistics continue to show disproportionate distributions of income and wealth between racial groups, as one social barometer after another mirrors the dismal state of black people in the poorest strata of our economic hierarchy, it is clear to me that the time for celebration must be postponed. (September 25, 1997; full text in appendix.)

My response was not popular. There were many who expressed dismay that I would voice such sentiments. On the same page in the *Democrat-Gazette,* just below my contribution, there was a statement by one of the former white students from Central who is now a practicing lawyer in Arkansas. He argued that we had forgotten that the crisis at Central was not just about the Little Rock Nine, that there were white students there as well. He went on to say that most of the white students wanted the nine of us to be there and that only a few students opposed our presence.

This is not the way I remember it. Official reports, personal testimonies, archival footage from news services, newspaper reports, photos, documents, and my own experiences contradict his account of the events. History cannot be rewritten in the face of overwhelming evidence to the contrary.

But that does not deter those who seem convinced that things were not at all what they seemed to be. The lawyer is not alone in his contention that some of us have it wrong. According to him and others, the truth is that there were only a few deluded souls standing in the way of progress in racial affairs in Little Rock. To them, "good" white people wanted to embrace not only the nine of us but any and all black children who wanted to enroll in Central High. And this, in part, is why it is not yet time for celebration. As long as voices such as these continue to offer their points of view for public consideration, our task, as I see it, is to work toward establishing some kind of reasonable level of awareness about what did happen in 1957 and to use that honest account as a starting point for making real change.

17

Consulting for the Little Rock School District

In May 1998, I was hired as a desegregation consultant by the Little Rock School District. During my four-year stint as consultant for the Little Rock School District, I bumped into many of my former white classmates from Central who are now employed by the district. Almost to a person, they denied having caused me harm or injury, essentially saying, "I didn't do it." I had finally met all the non-participants in the program of harassment that I remembered from Central!

In one encounter, a white woman told me that I had caused her to miss her prom; she had planned for an entire year, picking out her dress and her date, but because of the integration, no prom was scheduled in 1958. It was evident from her tone and from the fierce look on her face that she was still upset about this. On another occasion, I was approached by a man in the Little Rock Airport who identified himself as having been in my physical education class at Central. As he said that, I involuntarily took a step or two backward, recalling the hell I had gone through in that class. He quickly assured me that he was not one of the ones beating me up in 1957, but he was one of those standing by while I was being beaten. He introduced me to his son with whom he was traveling to a music conference. He said that he was sorry for his lack of backbone. He said that in the intervening years he had felt bad that he had been so cowardly. I quickly assured him I understood his plight and that I was aware of the social sanctions that would have been brought to bear against him had he tried to defend or help me. He asked for forgiveness and offered his hand in friendship. Unfortunately that kind of encounter is rare. Most of those feelings go unspoken and so remain unresolved.

As part of my consultation duties in the school district, I led seminars, conducted workshops, and talked with personnel in the district about problems associated with diversity. I visited schools to see for myself what the real issues and problems looked like from school to school. As one might expect, this led to my discovering a number of things unrelated to the district's efforts to desegregate. One very memorable discovery was the method used by the district's security forces to search for contraband goods—including drugs and weapons—that kids might have brought to campus.

In unannounced raids, teams would swoop into classrooms and order all of the students to line up for inspection. A full body search would be conducted on each kid followed by an inspection of backpacks or other bags belonging to the kid in question, and finally, a search of each student's locker. I was inside a classroom in one of the district's middle schoools on the day of one of these gestapo-like raids, and I was shocked at how the entire episode unfolded.

The team of four people rushed in and, without identifying themselves, started giving orders to the students to line up one row at a time while the other students were to remain seated. I was sitting in one of the rows of seats but was told by one of the security people that I didn't have to be searched. I suppose the person recognized me and decided that it would not be a good idea to include me in this process. I insisted, however, that I be treated just as the students were being treated. I was outraged that this was happening at all, but especially because a large number of the middle schoolers were terrified. Many of them were sixth graders who would have been in elementary schools had the district not changed the way in which schools were organized.

In that year, middle schools had been redesigned to include sixth graders. I saw in the eyes of these frightened young people a terror that caused me no small amount of mental and emotional anguish.

I took my place in line as my row was called and suffered along with the students the indignity of being searched and having the electronic wand passed over my body. Already I was forming the complaint I would make to the district authorities. I asked the team conducting the searches if this was standard operating procedure and they told me it was. I contained my rage, sensing that these middle school students did not need to have another adult "going off" in their presence. The team of security personnel had already yelled and screamed at them enough. I didn't want to add yet another layer to their anxiety.

I went straight to the district office that afternoon and lodged my offical complaint about the tactics I had seen employed at the middle school. I remember being stopped in mid-sentence by the official I had cornered. He informed me that the district's attorneys had reviewed the procedures and had assured all concerned that the district was well within the law to conduct such unannounced searches. I countered by saying I had no doubt whatsoever that this was the case. I said, "My concern is not whether the law was broken; my concern is the impact these tactics had on the kids. I was there, I saw their faces, I saw the terror in their eyes and watched as they tried to deal with the uncertainty of the situation." Finally, after more ranting on my part and more attempts on their part to persuade me that no laws had been broken, they said, "Maybe you should plan some kind of training session for the security force."

I should not have been surprised by any of this, neither the raid nor the response from the official, because much of what I had seen in the district during my tenure as consultant had been a consistent effort to hide behind the letter of the law. And now I was being told essentially, "If you want any change, you will have to do it." This was better than nothing, so I arranged to meet with the director of security, and we agreed on a day and time that I would train the security officers in more humane methods.

As I worked as a consultant for the district, I concluded that racist attitudes were widespread. This realization gave me a place to start in my efforts to help the district understand how to cope with difference. It led me to submit a plan for mandatory training in coping with difference for *everyone* who worked in the Little Rock School District.

The plan was received and acknowledged, but when I did not hear from anybody about its implementation for nine months, I decided to ask for a spot on the agenda for the regular school board meeting to give an update about my activities as consultant. I was granted the time, and I gave a fairly comprehensive accounting of all I had been doing up to that time. At the end of my report I mentioned the plan I had submitted nine months earlier. I briefly outlined my plan. I asked for a six-month commitment and an intensive two-day workshop for all employees of the district. After providing a few more details about the plan, I reminded them that I had submitted the plan nine months before, but I had heard nothing from the district office since then. The school board meetings were televised on local cable, so I hoped some interest might be generated by my remarks.

I was right. When I returned to my room at the Capital Hotel, the phone was ringing. School officials were angrily asking why I had called them out in such a fashion. They told me that people in Little Rock who had seen the telecast were already asking questions about this plan I mentioned. I responded by asking them when we might start the training program.

I got the go-ahead to implement the training program. We started a process of implementation shortly after my televised appearance at the board meeting. The first part of the activity included my identifying personnel in the district who would be willing to learn how to administer the training. Once that crew was identified, we spent several weeks going over the details of the program. Teams of two were assigned to present the training program under my overall supervision. The main thrust of the program was the participants' personal growth. I was committed to altering the misguided assumptions that participants used to navigate the racial terrain of their lives.

Following the two-day intensive workshop, participants were asked to publicly state their plans for continued growth and development over the coming six months. I chose to have them share their plans in this way because I knew that people are more likely to do something if they have publicly avowed they will do it. We were able to train approximately six hundred people before the district was released, in 2002, from federal supervision.

This judicial decision, however, brought the training activity to an abrupt halt. Although I had assurances from the superintendent that efforts to change the attitudes of district personnel would continue without the federal mandate, I knew they would not. I told the superintendent what I thought would happen, and it turned out I was right. I had predicted that if the court ruled in the district's favor, I would no longer be called upon to serve as a consultant.

I was called to testify at the court hearing when the school district took its case into federal court. In preparation for my appearance I spoke with John Walker, one of the attorneys for the plaintiffs in the ongoing case against the district. I asked him what he thought would happen if the court ruled for the plaintiffs. "We will get due process," he told me, "but we will not get equal protection."

As he spoke these words, my mind reviewed an image I have carried around for many years. During the 1960s I chanced across a cartoon depicting a scene from a Southern courtroom. In the one-panel cartoon there is a jury comprised solely of white males, all of whom are laughing uncontrollably. The foreman is reading aloud to the judge the jury's verdict. The cartoon's caption reads: "Yo' honor, here come de punch line, NOT GUILTY!!" Obviously, a white defendant had been on trial for a civil rights violation. The plaintiff in that case got due process, his or her case was presented to the court, but equal protection was not a part of the legal bargain.

As I waited my turn to testify in the district's court case, my eyes wandered around the room, and suddenly it hit me: I was staring into the faces of all the past justices of the court. Their portraits were arrayed along the walls, and they all stared back at me in silent, monochromatic assent that this was *their* courtroom, not mine.

I considered each of the white male faces, and I began to imagine the court filled with eager fourth graders on a field trip to learn about American justice. They would sit in these same seats; they would have the vantage point that was mine; they would see these same faces staring at them. Some of them might wonder, *Why are they all men? Why are all the men white?* In truth, however, I knew my imaginary fourth graders were unlikely to think of these questions. By fourth grade, children have already been indoctrinated to accept this situation as normal. I knew that some of them would leave the courtroom feeling a sense of unease, probably a bit of cognitive dissonance, but I also knew that nobody would address the issue and help them understand how such a collection of portraits came to be. The fourth graders would leave at the end of their field trip with an incomplete view of American justice. They would know little if anything about the circumstances that helped to create that wall of portraits. But they would leave with what I have come to call the "national narrative" more firmly implanted in their young minds: that America has always been the land of the free and the home of the brave, and never, certainly, a place that would harbor notions of white superiority.

Before my appearance in the courtroom, one of the district's officials decided to speak candidly to me about what he deemed to be business as usual in the district. It was his assessment that the Little Rock School District did not care much about meeting the goals of school integration. He felt the real focus was on providing safe schools for white students so business and industry could be satisfied that if they wished to move their businesses to Little Rock, the children of their employees would have good schools to attend.

I thanked the official for his candor and upon reflection could see how he could come to such a conclusion. My own observations of district actions and responses tended to support his way of thinking. In fact, when I finally made it to the stand in the courtroom, I spoke about this issue and related what the official had shared with me. Some of his collegues who were in the courtroom that day were chagrined, and perhaps a bit angry, that I had chosen to include those comments in the public record. But the truth is the truth.

18

MUCH TO LEARN

We have much work to do to end racist practices in this country. The purveyors of white supremacy in Little Rock were unwilling to entertain the notion of accepting nine young black children into a school they saw as a place for whites only. They could see the need to confront us with hostility, but accepting us was indeed a foreign notion. And even remembering the degree to which those sentiments were held, I am still convinced we have the know-how to end racism, but, sadly, I feel we lack the will.

Several years ago I attended a meeting convened by a group called "Beyond War." This group was formed to ask this question:

> Since we humans have developed enough firepower to blow up the entire universe, why don't we stop now and consider how we might use the same brainpower we have employed to take us to the very edge of existence to figure out how to live in peace?

Extrapolating from their philosophy, I say, since we have proven how racist and exclusionary we can be, why don't we work now toward learning how to erase all the damaging lines of demarcation that keep us imprisoned in our racial, ethnic, and cultural enclaves?

We learned from Little Rock that keeping the lines in place prevents us from tapping our full human potential. We miss the opportunity to do all that we can do and be all that we can be. Much of my own energy during that time was used in the service of surviving—a truly basic human endeavor. What might I have been able to do if I had been able to use that energy in the service of higher-order pursuits?

I am convinced that I missed opportunities to build a more solid academic foundation simply because I was preoccupied with safety. I had to think hard about such mundane things as which door to use each morning at school. If I used the wrong door, I might walk into an ambush. If I failed to maintain a high level of vigilance each day, I might miss seeing an object being thrown at me. One day in English class, several can openers, the kind with sharp points for puncturing cans, were thrown at me. I immediately took the openers to the teacher, who looked at me increduously and said, "I didn't see it. Did you bring those in?"

Fortunately, not all classes were this bad. The English teacher who hadn't seen anything was just one of those people who felt that the old order had to be maintained.

It occurs to me that a much more effective use of our collective energy would be to figure out how to work together toward some more productive human objectives, some higher-order concerns. It is gratifying to know that mine is not the only voice continuing to speak to this issue. Lately I have read several books wherein the authors appeal to us to move beyond the ordinary in our interactions with each other, to remove the arbitrary boundaries between people that continue to characterize life in the twenty-first century.

Maurice Berger, in *White Lies*, makes a plea for the kind of intensive dialogue we need in order to demystify the dynamics of race. His memoir is one of many stories that can help us understand how we might proceed. James McPherson's memoir, *Crabcakes*, makes essential points about the interactions of different racial and cultural groups. And Albert Murray, in *South to a Very Old Place*, reminds us of the need to know as much as possible about the unfolding drama of race relations in this country.

If a dialogue is to begin, we will need to know as much as possible about what is going on. Each one of us needs to have a firm grasp of the essential elements involved. We need to have an informed historical perspective, some sense of the dynamics of racism as it is manifested today, and more importantly, where we are in our own thinking about these things. And since dialogue in this arena is often much more visceral than cerebral, we need to have some safe outlet for the emotions that will inevitably occur.

In writing about these matters, M. Scott Peck suggests that we live in a state of pseudo-community where actions are not congruent with beliefs, and if we are to create true community, we must go through the chaos of disrupting this false state of being. It will require, among other things, that we give up the fiction of "color-blindness" and really see each other as we are. The exchanges must be expressions of honest feelings and thoughts so that we can get to a level beyond fear, distrust, and anger, and use our collective power to find workable solutions to the problems we face.

19

Not a Linear Journey

"What do you do with your hatred toward white people?"

I considered this question very seriously, not only because the young white woman who asked me assumed that I must hate white people, but also because she was sincerely interested in knowing how I felt toward people like herself. She was a graduate student in sociology at UCLA, and I was the assistant dean of the UCLA School of Social Welfare. I had come there in 1985 for what was to be a nine-year stint as an administrator. The interview was part of a research project exploring the dynamics of racism, and I had been selected as a subject in part because of my background as one of the Little Rock Nine. My answer seemed to disappoint the young student.

I told her I did not have hatred toward white people. Her response startled me. She said, "I don't believe you. All black people must have some degree of hatred toward white people, having experienced the discrimination and prejudice so prevalent in this country." While I could, and did, agree with her about the racial climate in the United States, I told her once more that I did not hate white people. Convinced that I was lying to her, she ended the interview abruptly and left my office.

I have thought about that episode often since then and have concluded that the young woman was unable to fathom how one could be black in this country and not have strong negative feelings about all white people. Based on her knowledge of my experience in Little Rock, she was certain that I, perhaps more than some other black person, would have developed feelings of hatred.

As I write this, I am reminded of the question put to Miles Davis at one point in his career. A reporter asked him if he hated white people, and after a brief pause, he said, "Not all the time." Maybe it was something along these lines the UCLA student sought from me. In any case, she left with her perceptions intact and with the conviction that I had not been honest with her about my feelings.

She might have discovered if she had stayed around a while that I had made a conscious decision not to hate. This decision was in part a matter of listening yet again to my mom who told me, "You cannot afford to hate. You have only enough life force to sustain you for roughly eighty years of life, and if you use any of it in the name of hating others, you shorten that prospective life span, or at the least, you impair the quality of existence for however many years you do live. The person or persons you hate will contribute nothing to the cost. The full price must be borne by you."

All of that made sense to me. Why would I engage in any behavior that might interfere with my living a life of quality? And I might have reminded the student as well that my belief in Christian principles did not permit the harboring of hate.

Over these past fifty years since the desegregation of Little Rock's Central High School in 1957, I have had plenty of time to reflect upon my experiences there. Without doubt, what the nine of us experienced was hatred, hatred so raw and undisguised that it would have been hard to mistake it for anything else. Every day we faced racism in its most virulent forms as white high school students used the term *nigger* in as many ways as they could:

"Hey nigger, how much you weigh? If you fall into a bucket of shit, I want to know how much to dip out."

"Nigger, how do you know when to stop washing your face?"

"All niggers belong in Africa! Why don't you go back there?"

I can still hear the sound of those voices over the span of these fifty years, and I can see the faces, faces distorted and twisted by racial hatred into grotesque caricatures of human beings.

Although I was surrounded by hatred, I chose not to respond in kind. "But how were you, a fifteen-year-old kid, able to make such a choice?"—this question finds its way into most of the interviews where my experience at Central is the subject. The interviewers, no doubt remembering themselves at fifteen, cannot imagine anybody having enough restraint at that age to ignore the taunting. I quickly respond by saying, "It was not about ignoring; I was fully aware of what was being said and made mental notes so I wouldn't forget. But at the same time, I was aware that what was being said had nothing whatsoever to do with me."

Even as a fifteen year old I had learned that people tell you who *they* are by what they say to you. And also, what they say has absolutely nothing to do with you. The messages I was getting from many of the white kids at Central were clear, unmistakable statements that they were infected with racism.

I figured, too, that many of them were simply parroting what they had heard from parents, relatives, friends, and neighbors, not realizing that by doing so they were adopting those same perspectives. And this is the part that demands some scrutiny: They were unwilling to make up their own minds, but they allowed parents and others to do their thinking for them.

Most of all, I knew I could make choices based on who I was. I didn't have to choose based on who was around me or accept what they were saying about me as truthful or in any way definitive of who I was. Unlike some of my white peers, I was unwilling to simply parrot the language of racism and discrimination.

My choice to meet the evils of racism with calm, studied reason was, in part, a function of my basic personality. I was then, and am now, a fairly easy-going type, not known to explode in the face of irritating behavior or adverse circumstance. It takes a lot to make me angry. For example, a junior high classmate took great pleasure in thumping my head whenever he saw me. Perhaps he was fascinated by the fact that I usually wore my hair cut very close to the scalp. In any case, he seemed to be unable to resist sneaking up behind me and popping me on the head. To avoid him I changed my route to school repeatedly. I entered the building by different doors whenever possible. Each day I asked him to stop, and I appealed to the teachers. Finally one day I told him if he did it one more time, I would hurt him. This episode took place over several weeks, so a lot of heat was required to get me to that boiling point. Despite my warning, he continued to harass me and I did indeed have to hurt him: I jabbed a sharp number-two pencil into his left bicep after his *last* thump to my head.

Usually at Central I would not bother to respond. In fact, I could give the impression that the other person did not even exist. I knew deep within that if things ever got to the point where I felt fighting was inevitable, where I was willing to give up nonviolence as an option, I would act swiftly and decisively. This was probably a function of the great aversion to fighting that I had had for a long time.

As my junior high classmate can testify, I can be as fierce as the next person. And since I know that about myself, I am careful to avoid situations where my fear of fighting can result in someone else getting hurt.

Self-awareness may hold some of the answers about how best to resolve the significant racial issues our country faces. And it is not just awareness about potential reactions in the face of danger, but an overall high-level awareness about who we are and what we are all about. The kind of awareness I propose has to do with knowing as much as possible about the driving forces in your life. What are the compelling images that guide your thinking in response to others, especially others you deem to be different from you?

When I served as a consultant in Little Rock, I urged the participants in my mandatory training program to develop such levels of awareness about the thoughts and feelings that fueled their responses to others. Immediately upon the heels of this newly discovered awareness I invited the participants to consider making a commitment to applying what they had found in the process. I explained to them that awareness with no intention of using it was as worthless as no awareness. I told them that this was a fluid process that continued over a lifetime. It was something that had to be revisited continually if it was to be of any real use.

And as we explored the various levels of commitment, I explained that this was not a linear process, but rather one that required an ability to gain the balance required, inevitably lose it from time to time, but then be able to regain it when necessary. I shared with the various groups that this was something I used in my own life, and I could testify that it worked. When I was willing to make a commitment to use the newly found awareness, it was more likely than not that I would actually do something with the information I had gleaned.

We must continue to find ways to extricate ourselves from the bondage of racism and our tendency to discriminate based on race. Successful eradication of all vestiges of this cancerous growth on our society will not be easy, nor will there always be obvious road signs to direct our journey. If we are to succeed in confronting and eliminating racism in our culture, it will be through real commitment and consistent, determined, concentrated action. Do we have the motivation or desire to accomplish this feat? This is the first question, and it must be answered in the affirmative if we are to realize even one fraction of the goal before us. Certainly it will not be an assignment for the weak of heart or those with doubt-filled minds. But if the true visionaries among us take up the challenge, we can find a way to make it happen.

L ittle Rock proved to be a demanding learning environment for me. But it gave me opportunities to discover the tools I needed to continue to survive and even thrive in these United States of America. I learned, for instance, that I needed to know as much as possible about the way in which society was structured. I needed a ready grasp of the rationale used to maintain the lines of separation between groups of people, especially those lines drawn in color. When you have a fairly complete understanding of something, it is easier to figure out how to deal with it. Operating in the dark does not afford you much opportunity to make beneficial changes.

I also learned it was not going to be an easy task to persuade white people to give up power and control in the name of equality and justice. This reality led me to conclude I had better be prepared for a very long and difficult battle with an entrenched and resolute group of white people determined to maintain the status quo at all costs.

As young people in Little Rock in 1957 we faced a harsh reality. Hundreds of white citizens were dedicated to keeping us penned in racially defined enclaves and restricting our access to the corridors of social, political, and economic power. But this simply motivated us to try to change these prevailing conditions, to look for ways to access these benefits of citizenship that had been denied to us because of our race.

Our decision to enter Central High School was based primarily on the fact that none of the racial barriers constructed to keep the nine of us out of Central could be justified. The legal, social, economic, and psychological barriers remained in place simply because they were shored up by the posturing and self-interested concern of white people who continued to benefit from their presence. The foundations upon which the barriers were constructed were not solid enough to keep them in place in the face of our concerted effort to remove them. Even as young people, we believed it was time for new ways of thinking about how society could be constructed to allow for the full and complete participation of all people, not just white people.

The sad truth is that our decision to challenge what some saw as a sacred way of life prompted harsh responses from dedicated segregationists. From the continuous harassment we faced during the 1957-58 school year to the closing of all of Little Rock's high schools the following year, to the tumultuous years of the early 1960s at Central High where black students suffered unspeakable indignities, we saw the degree to which segregationists would fight to keep things from changing.

Today I find that too many of my fellow citizens are satisfied with what I call the "surface changes" in our society. The kind of chaos that erupted at Central in 1957 will likely not be repeated; real changes have occurred. But, in my estimation, the changes are largely cosmetic. Most of the obvious barriers to education, employment, housing, and political participation have been removed. There are no longer governors standing in schoolhouse doorways, no signs reading "No blacks or dogs allowed." But these attitudes and sentiments still exist. Individuals who have been steeped in segregationist traditions still wield power in many arenas. And systemic, institutional racism continues. It is not accidental, for instance, that the nation's prisons house a disproportionate number of black males, that the wealth gap between whites and blacks continues to widen, and that schools across the country are often more segregated today than they were in 1957.

At some point we must question these realities. It simply isn't true that black people are somehow unable to compete equally because they are racially inferior, or that they are more criminally inclined than white people, or that they simply don't take advantage of opportunities to build wealth. If you consider that between 1619 and 1954 it was considered perfectly legal to discriminate against black people in this country, that for 335 years black people were denied opportunities to compete with whites, it is easy to understand how much of our current social, educational, and political reality has been informed by historical precedent.

In 1954 the Supreme Court ruled that discrimination was no longer constitutional, but it has only been fifty-five years since that decision was rendered. Contrast the 335-year period with the fifty-four years we have enjoyed since *Brown*. It is not an easy task to reshape a society that was constructed using social and legal blueprints that pre-date *Brown*, especially in the face of the overt resistance to the *Brown* decision itself.

Little Rock taught me how grudgingly people accept the kinds of change we believed in and demanded. It is obvious that many of those who so violently opposed our efforts thought their lives of comfort and prosperity depended on maintaining racial segregation. They are still at work, and their efforts to maintain the lines of racial discrimination continue to interfere with the efforts of those who would remove the vestiges of racism which diminish the daily lives of people of color.

The "old school" voices are much more strident and demanding than any of the speakers of the new gospel. The private school movement in Little Rock is but one small example of this reality. Rather than support a truly integrated public school system, many citizens are willing to provide the financial capital and other resources to build mono-racial schools so that their children can avoid association with "inferior" others.

And, to further muddy the waters, we have such high-profile voices as Bill Cosby and Juan Williams who would have us believe that black people are solely responsible for their plight, that the lack of education and the absence of wealth is evidence of sloth and inability to take advantage of obvious opportunities. They base their positions only on their own personal experiences. This is not surprising because most of us understand the world through our own experiences, thinking, *If it happened this way for me, it can, or even should, happen this way for you.* What Cosby and Williams forget, as do Shelby Steele, Ward Connerly, Clarence Thomas, and others who have had similar experience, is that black people and people of color in general, are unequally oppressed in this society. One's personal success is never a matter of individual effort; it is a process that involves countless decisions by many others, and the fact that you have "made it" is testimony to the fact that those decisions, in concert, proved favorable. Yes, the individual makes decisions as well, but it is the combination of circumstances and the confluence of fortuitous events that dictate the outcome.

These newly appointed spokesmen seem to forget also that history matters. In some of their public statements you find references to the idea that we are using "outdated notions of structural racism." I contend that history, all of history, is but the antecedent action to all we find around us today. The "notions" cannot be outdated simply because they began at some earlier point in our chronological lives. We must determine the extent to which societal structures continue to limit access and opportunity to people who have been traditionally denied access and opportunity. It is irresponsible to take the position that such realities are non-existent.

The Little Rock Nine faced formidable barriers and unspeakable indignities as a result of institutionalized practices. In the face of legal and ultimately physical force, the segregationists gave way only to regroup and develop more insidious ways to maintain their chosen way of life. This was but a microcosm of what happens even today as we continue to struggle with many of the same issues that were prevalent in 1957.

I write not as one who wishes to "live in the past" but as one who wishes to understand how the past is manifest today. I choose not to join the chorus of those who say that we must forget what happened and get on with life. I am firmly convinced that we will fail to accomplish our goal of creating a truly integrated and equal society if we continue to avoid facing the truth about who we are and have been. We must face our past with unflinching honesty if we are to determine the most appropriate next steps for our future.

During the time I worked in the Los Angeles County Department of Child Welfare, the prevailing logic was that we should attempt to find the best possible situation for children who were wards of the court. Most of them were so designated because either one or both parents were absent from their lives. At some point it was determined that the best possible circumstance was something that could not be achieved, since the parents were not present. It was then decided that our focus would be to find the *least detrimental available alternative.* I think we can use that approach as we consider how to remedy the situation we face in terms of the imbalanced social, legal, and political realities of our lives. We can find the least detrimental available alternative and count that as the starting point in our quest to discover what truly can be done to bring resolution to the myriad problems we face.

THE LITTLE ROCK NINE FOUNDATION

In 1997 during the observation of the forty-year anniversary of the events in Little Rock, the nine of us formed a non-profit foundation. The foundation awards scholarships to young people all over the world who need financial assistance to complete post-high school educational programs. Additionally we offer consultation to school districts about issues related to school desegregation and will eventually host forums to discuss these and other related items.

You can find more information about the foundation at www.littlerocknine.org. I encourage you to visit the site to learn more about the foundation and to see if there are ways in which you might join us in this endeavor. Carlotta Walls Lanier is president of the foundation. If you have thoughts or ideas about our work, please feel free to direct your comments to her.

Philander Smith College Remarks
by Terrence J. Roberts, Ph.D.
Member, Little Rock Nine
Saturday, September 27, 1997

A s I stand in this spot I can see down Izard Street where I lived as a young boy growing up in Little Rock. Coming to the campus at Philander Smith College was on my playtime agenda as my friends and I climbed these steps and slid down these banisters. I am on familiar ground today. Later, Philander Smith was to provide much needed services to me and my eight colleagues when we were denied entrance to Central High School in September, 1957. During the three-week period as we awaited the outcome of the legal wrangling over states' rights versus federal rights, Philander Smith College faculty and students tutored us in the high school subjects being taught to our future Central High classmates. From these dedicated educators and scholars we heard the same litany that had been communicated to us by teachers at Gibbs Elementary, Stevens Elementary, Dunbar Junior High School, and Horace Mann High; they told us in words chosen carefully to accentuate the message that education was important and that excellence was the expectation. They continued to do this for the entire academic year of 1958-59 as well when all Little Rock public high schools were closed in the name of "segregation forever," and African-American students were in need of educational resources.

Earlier today I spoke to a group of Philander Smith students and urged them to take the educational process seriously, to resist the impulse to follow pathways that might lead them away from the center of the educational arena, and to accept the mantle of learner with all of its attendant requirements. The foremost one of which is the choice to commit at the "fifth level," to do whatever it takes to succeed. The first level of commitment is embodied in the reply, "I'll think about it." Not much commitment even hinted at here. Following is the second level, "I'll try," which is not much better than the first. The next level, "I'll do what I can," seems to promise more, but it too is empty of substance. The fourth level describes the degree of commitment given by the legalist, the one who follows the letter of the law. This person will do only that which is required, not an iota more. It is the fifth level that demands total involvement. It was a fifth level commitment that we took to Central High School.

This commitment enabled us accept the restrictions placed upon us as we sought to educate ourselves in an unfriendly, hostile environment. The school officials demanded that we, the Little Rock Nine, not participate in extracurricular activities while we were in school as a condition of our enrollment. The manifest reason was that our safety could not be ensured. Given that we had the backing of the 101st Airborne Division of the United States Army, I am forced to conclude that there was probably a latent rationale for this decision. And one such possible explanation would be that by keeping us segregated within this milieu we would not reap the intangible benefits that accrue to those who are free to form whatever associations they choose and that might enhance the developmental process. The development of contacts that extend beyond the high school corridors and which could translate into admission to better colleges, jobs with better potential for advancement, the transfer of information necessary for the building of substantive social networks—all of this and more that might result from the unfettered association that an open society demands, the kind of affirmative action that has always existed for white Americans, but which has been systematically denied to black Americans. In his book, *The Birth and Death of Meaning*, Ernest Becker penned these words which have become one of my favorite phrases to quote: "It is the task of culture to provide each and every individual with the firm conviction that he or she is an object of primary value in a world of meaningful action." This community failed in its obligation to me in 1957. Finally, after military force was applied, I was offered a shadow, but little substance. Years ago a friend of mine said that the taste of honey is bitter when niggardly given by the lily white hand that beats you; I think he was on to something.

In the past few days several of us have made public statements about the need to focus on access as we think about the integration of schools. I would like to reiterate that and to add that we are talking about total access. We want it all. We don't want just a taste. In order to facilitate the healthy growth and development of African-American children in this multi-racial, multi-ethnic, multi-lingual society, we need to give them the chance to communicate and interact with everybody else. The same is true for white youngsters as well. It would be unfortunate if our remarks were misconstrued in any way to suggest that we were against the desegregation of schools. The Little Rock Nine stands firmly committed to the desegregation of schools. We know that Little Rock's schools remain under federal orders to desegregate; this has been the case since 1956, forty-one years ago. We are aware of the school district's latest proposal to have the eighth circuit court of appeals approve their revision of the desegregation plan which would remove court supervision by the school year 2001. To that I would simply say, if what the Little Rock School District plans to do has merit, if, in fact, the plan is based on principles of equality for all students regardless of color or ethnicity, the results will stand the scrutiny of any overseeing body even beyond the year 2001. Obviously, the step we took in 1957 has not been followed by the necessary additional steps to ensure that all school children in this city have maximum opportunity to realize the potential that is theirs.

In the exhibition in the state capitol rotunda that presents the rich history of Dunbar Junior High School, there is a section where one can read about the language routinely printed on diplomas awarded to graduating students. It is written that the holder of this diploma qualifies for entrance into Little Rock Central High School, but the rules of segregation were so well entrenched that no students graduating from Dunbar ever concluded that attendance there was possible. To structure a society in such a manner robs all of its citizens of opportunities to grow and prosper in the truest sense. For many African Americans, leaving Little Rock was the only viable pathway to academic and professional success. The tragedy of that reality is reflected in the disintegration of families and the loss of social frameworks that would have included the formal and informal transfer of knowledge and information between and among African Americans at each end of and along a wide continuum. The security of having an established home base with a loving extended family and a school system where you are cherished and expected to succeed fits well with Becker's notion about the task of culture. If the Little Rock School District would like to move beyond the confines of restricted thinking into a realm of fifth level commitment to the highest ideals, they can start using all available energy to figure out how to make Becker's idea real in the school system. Jonathan Kozol, in his preface to *Death at an Early Age*, says that the most pernicious thing an adult can do to a child is to meet him or her with minimal expectations. When my own children were in grade school, they told me about a classmate whose parents had given her a dollar for each grade of A she earned. My reply was that since going to school was their main job, their primary chore, then they would owe me a dollar for each class in which they did not earn the grade of A. It was all about levels of expectations.

Sitting to my right is a man I met in 1987 when he was governor of Arkansas. I remember coming home to share with my wife that I had met a man who seemed to "get it." He appeared to understand this country's need to confront the issues of race and racism. Now, as president, Bill Clinton has established a commission to explore the dynamics of race and racism which I hope will lead us all to a fifth level commitment to do whatever it takes to move this country beyond the narrow confines of racial prejudice and discrimination into the realm of peer relationships where each person is honored and embraced without imposed conditions. It is my expectation that we will indeed take the opportunity that is ours to structure a society for the twenty-first century that offers all citizens the right to exist unfettered by the restrictions of racist ideology or its nefarious soulmate, the notion of white supremacy. Until each person is free to follow the pathways suggested by inherent potential, none of us is truly free.

And now, it is my privilege and pleasure to present to you our next speaker, President William Jefferson Clinton.

The Ongoing Battle for Equality
by Terrence J. Roberts, Ph.D.
Arkansas Democrat-Gazette
Thursday, September 25, 1997

According to some contemporary sources, the modern African-American civil rights struggle finds its genesis in Rosa Parks' refusal to give up her Montgomery, Alabama, bus seat to a white man on Dec. 1, 1955. From there, according to these same sources, the struggle moved to Little Rock, Arkansas, in 1957 when nine black children needed the might of the 101st Airborne Division of the U.S. Army to enter the previously all-white Central High School.

Those events, as poignant as they were, did not occur in a vacuum. They were skirmishes in the ongoing battle for equality, fought tenaciously by enslaved Africans and African Americans throughout the history of this country. African slave men, women, and children worked amidst the cruelest conditions possible to build an economically strong America. At the same time, they sought full participation in the body politic as economic, political, and social equals. Many black people sacrificed their lives so that succeeding generations might have opportunities to maximize inherent potential without the threat of oppression.

When I consider that the battle rages still in 1997, I realize that I have no time for celebration. Time for reflection, yes. Time for remembering the past so the future can be better informed, yes. But as Little Rock's schools remain under federal orders to desegregate, as affirmative action programs are being dismantled across the country, as statistics continue to show disproportionate distributions of income and wealth between racial groups, as one social barometer after another mirrors the dismal state of black people in the poorest strata of our economic hierarchy, it is clear to me that the time for celebration must be postponed.

This year President Clinton appointed a seven-member commission to establish a national dialogue about things racial in the United States. This action I applaud, for it has long been my contention that the chief executive, by setting the necessary tone, can help this country find the will and commitment to end racism and the accompanying ideology of white supremacy. Despite our long history of fighting racist forces in education, employment, housing, transportation, and other arenas, racism is very much alive in America. Despite the claims of some that classism, not racism, is the issue, we African Americans are faced with racist actions, attitudes, and consequences every day of our existence. Starting a dialogue about this would serve to move us eventually from the visceral, reactionary stage to the level of cognitive engagement where we can develop strategies and mechanisms designed to eradicate every vestige of this consuming evil.

Many times I have been asked, "Don't you think we have made progress?" "Why do we still have to talk about racism?" "Can't we just be color-blind?" The questioners often are ready to celebrate what they see as stellar accomplishments and accuse me of being oversensitive and paranoid. I cannot, in good conscience, celebrate what some would label progress while so many of my fellow citizens of color remain oppressed.

In 1957 it was the goal of the Little Rock Nine to simply integrate a school. Our task was to take our places in the trenches to carry on the fight against forces that sought to relegate black people to the back of the bus, the back of the employment line, the back door. The task we all face today is not how to integrate schools but how to educate children of all ethnicities to think beyond the narrow confines of racist ideology. Our goal today is not to enrich ourselves so that we can encircle our necks with bands of South African gold but to invest the profits signaled by the rising Dow-Jones in ways that promote a vision for the twenty-first century untrammeled by thoughts mired in our racist past.

As a young boy growing up in Little Rock, I was convinced that there must be a place somewhere that was not governed by the same rules that restricted my freedom in so many ways. As an adult, I have concluded that such a place can exist, but it will require concerted effort on the part of large numbers of American citizens. I have made the trek back to Little Rock this week to take part in the activities associated with the observance of the passage of forty years since the initial desegregation of Central High. Some have talked of reconciliation as we remember those times and those events. I would simply remind those who speak in such terms that to be reconciled there must have been some friendship or harmony then in existence that can now be restored. Perhaps it would be more fruitful to talk about how we can confront the past and learn from it, and in so doing begin to build a future devoid of those structures created to place white people at the top of some mythical racial hierarchy.

We must remember that it was the governor of Arkansas, with the complicity of the people, who closed all of the public high schools in Little Rock during academic year 1958-59, an act so egregious that forty years later, many who might have earned a high school diploma have not done so. We must recall that it took yet another Supreme Court decision, *Cooper vs. Aaron*, to force the governor to open the schools. It was the voice of the White Citizens' Council that expressed so much open disdain for black citizens. It was the "average" white citizen, not some demented, deluded interloper, who filled the ranks of the mobs surrounding Central High.

We need to understand exactly how and why all of this happened so that it can be avoided in the future. In David Augsburger's insightfully written book, *Caring Enough to Confront*, we find his thesis that those who care enough will confront the issues pertinent to the relationship. If we care enough about the relationships between and among all the people of Little Rock, we have to confront the salient issues. And the chaos that engulfed us in 1957 has left us with a legacy of significant issues to be confronted.

I write these words from the fund of information that shapes my mental map, the guide I use to make sense of the world around me. In the ideal, I would write about some subject of compelling and general interest arising out of my unencumbered exploration of the universal terrain, but because of the reality we share, a reality marred by a plethora of racist decisions and consequences, I write in the name of civil rights for all people. It is my hope that we will have reasons to engage in the joyful celebration of full and complete freedom for black people in this country. Indeed, the time for celebration may come, but make no mistake, it has not yet arrived.

Nine Who Dared

The Little Rock Nine dared to do what many felt was impossible to do, and what an even larger number felt was wrongheaded and ill-advised at best. In the following words I wish to offer my tribute to eight of the most courageous people I know, young people who possessed great resolve and unswerving conviction that it was time to make radical changes to a system that threatened to rob us all of any opportunity to develop the potential inside of us waiting to be realized. It was a time that demanded clear thinking and a readiness for action, a willingness to question the efficacy of a status quo that held few possibilities for large numbers of people simply because they were defined as African-American.

This small group came together as a result of the confluence of ideas and principles that together spelled the near end of the system of racial apartheid in America. Sensing a need to communicate in no uncertain terms to all who would listen that they were willing to die if necessary in the cause of freedom, the Little Rock Nine raised the bar for all of us. It is my wish in these following paragraphs to give you some measure of insight into the character and mindset of my eight colleagues.

Ernest Green

It seems natural to start this tribute with a message about the lone senior in our group, Ernest Green, affectionately known among us and his large circle of friends and acquaintances as Ernie. Years before Central High School was ever on our collective radars, Ernie had established himself as a young man with abundant ambition and a vision of the future that held no limits for him. Easygoing in manner, Ernie was always the picture of relaxed, anxiety-free existence in a world where disruptive elements threatened to intrude at any moment. His ability to see beyond the craziness, to imagine consequences and conclusions that defied the prevailing logic of the day, gave him an aura that helped to push aside concerns about imminent threats or fear that somehow things might get out of control.

Ernie's ability to get to the heart of any matter, to speak directly to the essence of whatever is being considered, is legendary. His raspy-voiced delivery adds a quality of earthiness that quickly gets your full attention. He sprinkles his comments with just enough expletives to fine tune the points he wishes to make. Even the most prudish among us is left feeling sanguine about any encounter with Ernie, especially when he is in "rare form" as he attacks one or more of the important issues of the day.

Earlier, I wrote about the summer of 1958 when Ernie and I lived and worked in New York. During that time period I was able to experience over a more concentrated period how balanced an approach to life Ernie takes. When the landlady's husband confiscated the rent money we had left for her, Ernie was unperturbed, and we eventually resolved the matter without undue upset. This is but one example of how Ernie meets life's exigencies. And it was, in part, this quality that allowed him to model for all of us how to navigate the uneven terrain of Central High.

I would say of Ernie that he embodies qualities that any of us would readily embrace and make our own. His love of people, his appreciation of the finer things in life, his unabashed joy expressed in hearty laughter, his family loyalty, all these and many more are accurate descriptors of a man I am proud to call friend and colleague.

Minnijean Brown Trickey

The word that comes quickly to mind when I think about Minnijean is exuberant. If you have ever seen someone who might be characterized as having a zest for life, you may have seen Minnijean. From my earliest recollections, this young woman has expressed, in action and speech, a joyous connection with the best life has to offer. It came as absolutely no surprise to me that the white students at Central manifested a decided aversion to Minnijean based on their conclusion that she really felt as if she belonged in their company. This was, in fact, true. Minnijean saw those students as peers, not better than or less than herself, just peers. And this was most upsetting to the white students who wanted to hold on to notions of white superiority.

When you spend time talking to Minnijean about issues of importance, you are instantly aware that you are in the presence of one who has thought deeply about such things. She is not one to gloss over substantive concerns. She has a point of view and wants to know how you have arrived at your own assessment of whatever happens to be the subject of discourse. It might be the case for some that they feel a bit intimidated by Minnijean's insistence on delving deeper into the problem, issue, concern, or theoretical supposition, but by staying in the dialogue, it is most certain that learning will take place.

One of the sheer pleasures in life for me is to be on the same platform with Minnijean as we engage audiences in discussions about things related to Little Rock. I know in advance that I will come away from those experiences with new perspectives, new ways of thinking about the past, the present, and the future. This is especially true as it relates to interactions across lines of racial or cultural demarcation. Witty, and quick to respond with in-depth assessments, Minnijean brings a measure of intellectual excitement to what too often become dull repetitions of platitudes or hackneyed phrases.

Perhaps more than anything, Minnijean is a person who practices inclusion in her daily life. She enjoys being in your company and communicates both verbally and nonverbally that she is willing to meet you on your own turf. You will not find in her a ready repository for items of gossip or unmerited summations about others; she is focused on life that transcends the ordinary, mundane exchange of juicy tidbits that some find to be the core around which their lives are built.

I like most about Minnijean that she stands up for principle. As a group, we all felt a warm glow inside when Minnijean decided to return the blows, to fight, literally, for her right to walk the halls of Central unimpeded by the actions of others. We did not see her response as abandonment of our choice to be nonviolent; to us it was a matter of knowing which hill to die upon. Perhaps she was motivated by the same sentiment that led Malcolm X to declare: "Ballots if possible, bullets if necessary." Inside, at the core of our being, we cheered loudly and long; Minnijean had done what we all wanted to do.

Elizabeth Eckford

Elizabeth walked alone on that fateful first day, and she suffered what may have been to a less able person a crushing psychological blow. In truth, she was, figuratively, knocked down by the experience, but she has risen. As I write these words I am reminded of Maya Angelou's poem "Still I Rise," in which she writes in lyric elegance about the ability of black women to rise above the fray to reach heights of their own choosing. Refusing to be beaten down by the forces of racism or the demeaning attitudes of others, these stalwart females stride forward with grace and purpose ever aware of the dangers around them but confident in their ability to defang or declaw as needed, whatever the situation demands. Elizabeth is one such person; she walks softly, but carries a big stick.

The adjective most of us would quickly apply to Elizabeth is shy. We see her as one who would prefer not to be in the center of action. But, in our haste to label her, we miss the fact that she simply wants the time to herself to evaluate and analyze the situation as it emerges before her. When she does speak up it is with the voice of authority. Behind that veil of reticence to engage we find the proverbial steel-trap mind ready and able to take on all comers. She demonstrates consistently an ability to synthesize disparate elements of an argument and distill them to their essence whether it be truth she discovers or whether she exposes the fallacies hiding among the carefully constructed verbiage.

That image you no doubt know well is the same one I see when I think about Elizabeth's most public display of courage under fire. As she makes her way south on Park Street in front of Central High School in 1957, she speaks to generations to come about what it takes to maintain dignity and poise in the face of unrestrained psychological assault. Her mask of serenity is belied, of course, by the churning emotions inside, but her ability to portray a sense of unruffled self-control is instructive to all of us.

Elizabeth has shown as well that she has the willingness to forgive those who were self-defined as her enemy during those hateful days at Central High. Her dialogues with Hazel Bryant, a person who describes herself as having been "the poster child for American racism," reveal a deep sense of commitment to higher ideals of existence. Elizabeth would not wish for herself or anybody else to be bogged down with resentments or unresolved emotions; she simply feels that it is better to rise above them. And, by so doing, Elizabeth has left a legacy that will continue to enrich the lives of human beings as we march, however uncertainly, into the future awaiting us.

Thelma Mothershed Wair

It is no secret to anyone that Thelma was the focus of much of our concern during the uproar at Central. Will her heart hold out, will she be able to withstand the daily attacks, will she have the stamina to survive this ordeal? These were the questions we asked ourselves and discussed together when we had time to do so. Thelma had suffered rheumatic fever as a young girl, and this debilitating illness had left her with a mortal frame that might make her more vulnerable to the physical violence we expected to endure, or so we thought. Thelma had other ideas. What she may have lacked by way of physical strength, she more than made up for by her strength of will and commitment to being at Central. Small in stature, Thelma towered over most all of her white student peers by virtue of her belief in the higher principles governing human interaction.

Thelma came from a very supportive family, as you might well imagine, and she took the energy they loaned to her as part of her recommended daily allotment for use each day at school. The rest of us benefited from this arrangement as well because as we watched Thelma find ways to manage the chaos around us, we were energized anew and found pockets of courage we hadn't known about until that time of discovery.

There is a descriptor used often about some people who seem to possess certain qualities, but I am ambivalent, at best, about its use. However, I am willing, in Thelma's case, to put aside my reservations and wholeheartedly endorse the use of this term as it applies to her. She is sometimes called "sweet." I think my hesitation to fully embrace this identifier is based on my conclusion that in most cases it is a way of saying that the person so described has very little to offer other than a pleasant disposition. That is patently not true in Thelma's case. True, her disposition is pleasant, but to end the discussion of her attributes at that point would be unjust and based on faulty intelligence.

Thelma is one of the sweetest people on the planet, in the truest sense of the word. She exudes a honeyed aura enhanced by the hint of a Southern accent in the lilt of her oratory. But all this aside, she is tough as nails in the trenches. Thelma not only survived the ordeal at Central, but after training to become an educator of young minds, took a position in the public school system in East St. Louis, Illinois. To me, that is *the* paramount example of going from the frying pan into the fire. She spent a career in that environment, retiring only recently to return once again to Little Rock and her supportive family. Thelma knows "what ought to be done" and she is willing to do it.

Melba Patillo Beals

Before we knew the word for it, before we even knew there was such a word at all, we knew that Melba was indeed a DIVA. We simply saw her as Melba Joyce, the one person in our world who could be counted on to know protocol, etiquette, proper responses, and how to couch putdowns in such elegant phrasing that the person so targeted never knew what had occurred. As a young girl in Little Rock, she was always first among equals when it came to matters of fashion or understanding complicated academic questions. This diva was not only a leader in things social, but "smart as a whip," as often concluded by those who assessed such matters.

Melba's well-rounded life included a lot of other things that were demonstrated by her involvement in school government, civic affairs, and church-related activities. It is no surprise at all that Melba chose to be included in our group of nine. For her, as it was for most of us, continuing to live under the oppressive conditions in Little Rock was simply untenable. Her sensibilities were offended by those who would assert that white people were superior to black people. There was nothing in Melba's world to support such an audacious pronouncement. In fact, there was an abundance of things to point to that proved to her that such an allegation was pure mendacity, totally without merit. Melba saw going to Central as a way of not only challenging the lie of white superiority, but providing opportunity for her to demonstrate what living a life of quality was all about.

While some might see in Melba's demeanor a measure of haughtiness, what I see mostly is her unwillingness to "suffer fools gladly." Melba does indeed demand that those in her world pay attention to the things that matter most. This is not to say that she is a soul without joy. Far from it! Melba enjoys life and laughs heartily along with the rest of us when the time for relaxation has arrived. Her way with words gives her an edge in that she is able to find the humor couched in some of life's more mundane activities and communicate her findings in creative patterns of speech. She is truly fun to be with!

Melba has the distinction of being the first of our group to write a book about her experiences at Central High. *Warriors Don't Cry* was published in 1994 and has been acclaimed as a memoir of the highest quality. In fact, I allude to her book in my use of the term "warrior" earlier in this book. Using her ability to create mind pictures in high definition, Melba takes the readers on a journey they will never forget. Lorene Cary, author of *Black Ice*, has this to say on the cover of Melba's book: "This story shows in clear detail that integration was war. Thanks to Ms. Beals for letting us walk with the young warriors from innocence to outrage and then through it all to understanding …. I want every young person I know to read this book."

Gloria Ray Karlmark

Gloria was one of three tenth graders in our small group in 1957. She and Jefferson Thomas and Carlotta Walls might be considered to be the "younger kids in the family." In fact, Gloria was the youngest child, by several years, in her family of origin which included two older siblings. Rumor has it that Gloria's parents were not keen on the idea of her enrolling at Central High and actually forbade her to do so. But in keeping with Gloria's penchant for following her own mind about things, she ignored this parental injunction and joined our group of nine. This would be portentous for a number of reasons, not the least of which is that Gloria was already well practiced in the art of doing what she pleased. As the favored younger child, she had the run of the household and used the opportunity to perfect her decision-making abilities.

This skill was on display at Central High in several ways. Gloria was simply not accustomed to following orders from others, so her response to the white kids at Central was basically to ignore much of their unsolicited and unwanted input. She was used to getting her way and was not about to allow the forces of opposition to deny her. This attitude, of course, led to some frustration for her, but she managed to find ways to cope.

It is my hunch that Gloria spent a great deal of her time at Central looking beyond the daily harassment to a future that she knew would not include having to deal with people who were limited in their ability to relate to different others. I say this because Gloria possesses an intellect that places her in the top five percent of the population. Her ability to think globally about issues then, as well as her continuing ability to do the same thing now, gives her a decided edge over those whose thought processes are less well-developed.

For the past several years Gloria has lived and worked in Europe; she currently lives in Sweden. And while I may be off track a bit, I feel certain that her decision to live abroad has as much to do with her frustration about lack of opportunity in this country as it has to do with her appreciation for the kind of life one can live in Sweden. In any case, she is one of the most interesting human beings in the universe. Her range of interests—from computer technology to stained-glass artistry—gives you a glimpse of her complexity.

Jefferson Thomas

You have to understand this about Jabbo: He is ever more ready to live with you in peace, but he has the heart of a lion. Keenly aware of his own ability to wreak havoc on your being, he restrains himself in the name of mutual harmony and domestic tranquility. It was a combination of these traits and his grounding in the tenets of Christianity that enabled him to embrace the principles of non-violence as we entered the battle zone of Central High School in 1957.

Jeff's subtle, engaging humor is one of his trademark qualities. He ropes you in with the promise of sober discourse and veers off to the inevitable punchline without so much as a warning turn signal. He gleams at you with delight pouring out of his twinkling eyes as you realize that his humor is but a mask for the cogent analysis that lies underneath. What you now have is so much more than the manifest content would have you believe. Homespun in manner and delivery, the razor-edged summation of whatever is the focus of *his* attention gets *your* attention.

One of three males in our group of nine teenagers who dared to challenge the Southern status quo, Jefferson was a high-profile target for the mean-spirited antagonists in Little Rock. He accepted this role without flinching, and earned the respect of a nation for his display of quiet courage in the face of extreme provocation.

Jeff knows the truth and is not afraid to live by its power. From the poem "Invictus" come these lines:

> In the fell clutch of circumstance
> I have not winced nor cried aloud.
> Under the bludgeonings of chance,
> My head is bloody, but *unbowed.*

And so I see Jeff, looking the enemy in the face without giving him the satisfaction of retaliation—rising above the level of animal savagery to embrace a more excellent way of being in this world.

Carlotta Walls Lanier

Mere words are sorely inadequate to describe this very talented and courageous woman. Who she is and what she represents in the universe is a call to the masters to create poetry, rhythm, symphonies, and artistic renditions in an attempt to capture her essence. And even then it is likely that the truth of her will remain unspoken in languages that we can understand, unheard by ears too clogged with the wax of banality, and unseen by eyes unaccustomed to the brightness of the light she sheds in her wake. I admit that such hyperbole may not seem warranted to some, but if you knew Carlotta, you too might be moved to such heights of expression. She possesses the kind of character and sense of justice that many of us strive to attain over the course of a lifetime. She is gracious, kind, loving, gentle, tactful, generous, and concerned about the welfare and well-being of others.

Carlotta is a natural leader of people, and she wears that mantle with an ease that belies the hard work and effort she expends in the name of exemplary leadership. Her attention to detail is such that management courses might be devised using her as the benchmark by which others might be measured. When you need a job done, and done well, call Carlotta. When you want to assure that your program will succeed, hire Carlotta to create the elements of success.

If it should fall your lot to be teamed with Carlotta in some enterprise, expect to move fast. Physical stamina is a must and mental acuity is a given, for in her world things get done with alacrity. She is not satisfied with half-done projects or poorly planned activities; so along with moving fast, you can expect that quality will not be sacrificed. But, although she is programmed to move at mach speed through the universe, Carlotta will not condemn you for not keeping pace with her. Something about her lets her know that others will not always be up to the tasks she sets for them, and she will make the necessary adjustments so that the team can jointly claim victory or join in celebration of a job well done.

Much earlier in this narrative I mentioned having breakfast with Carlotta and learning from her how she managed to deal with the insults and assaults at Central. Her reply was in keeping with my description of her in this section. She said, if you recall, that she knew better than to behave in those uncouth ways, but the white students did not. Yet there was no condemnation in her voice, just a simple observation of fact. That's Carlotta, aware of the reality around her but unwilling to allow the circumstances to dictate her response.

Carlotta is a trustworthy person, and that is a most important quality in this world of subterfuge and questionable ethical practices. You can depend on her to do what she says she will do and own up to any mistakes she might make. Carlotta is the kind of person you would most want to have as a friend and confidante. I feel privileged indeed to have had the opportunity to share space in the universe with Carlotta.

TERRENCE ROBERTS graduated from California State University, received an MSW degree from UCLA, and earned a PhD in psychology from Southern Illinois University. He now resides in California, where he owns and directs a management consulting firm. President Bill Clinton presented Roberts with the Congressional Gold Medal in 1999. Roberts is a frequent public speaker and has been featured on *Good Morning America*, *The Today Show*, *The Oprah Winfrey Show*, *The Rachel Maddow Show*, and *The Tavis Smiley Show*.

CPSIA information can be obtained
at www.ICGtesting.com
Printed in the USA
FFOW05n2326091017
40902FF